Eat & Explore
Washington

Eat & Explore

Washington

Favorite Recipes, Celebrations
& Travel Destinations

Christy Campbell

Great American Publishers
www.GreatAmericanPublishers.com
TOLL-FREE 1-888-854-5954

Great American Publishers

P. O. Box 1305 • Kosciusko, MS 39090

TOLL-FREE **1-888-854-5954 • www.GreatAmericanPublishers.com**

ISBN 978-1-934817-16-2

First Edition
10 9 8 7 6 5 4 3 2 1

by Christy Campbell

Front cover photo: Meadow, Wenatchee National Forest, Washington © Jupiterimages
Cover illustration: Mark P. Anderson, Big Whiskey Design Studio
Back cover photo: Courtesy of Crystal Mountain Resort
Back cover food image: Granny Smith Apple Pie p195 © Rez-art/thinkstock.com

Chapter opening photos: Appetizers & Beverages © Smokingdrum/istockphoto.com
Bread & Breakfast © Tannjuska/thinkstock.com • Soups & Salads © funwithfood/istockphoto.com
Vegetables & Other Side Dishes © Diana Didyk/istockphoto.com
Meat & Seafood © Ezhicheg/istockphoto.com
Desserts & Other Sweets © Edward ONeil Photography/istockphoto.com
Indexes © Christine Anderson Photography/thinkstock.com

Every effort has been made to ensure the accuracy of the information provided in this book.
However, dates, times, and locations are subject to change.
Please call or visit websites for up-to-date information before traveling.

To purchase books in quantity for corporate use, incentives, or fundraising,
please call Great American Publishers at 1-888-854-5954.

Contents

Introduction

Creating the EAT & EXPLORE STATE COOKBOOK SERIES is an inspiration. Not only does it inspire me to learn and experience more about the wonderful land in which I live, but there are unexpected moments of inspiration found in almost every aspect of everyday life. I travel between Mississippi and Louisiana quite often, and during my most recent trip I was thinking about Washington state… What is it like to live and work there? What is it like to travel between communities to visit family during special times? While asking myself these questions, the person being interviewed on the talk radio program I had playing began to talk about the Olympic Peninsula. This was it, my moment of inspiration. While listening, a picture began to form in my mind of living daily life with a majestic mountain ever present in the horizon. I imagined being able to plan a weekend trip to a temperate rain forest without having to board a plane. Lost in my thoughts about the Evergreen State, an image of a wonderful patchwork of color and culture was burned in my mind's eye.

The only state in the nation named after a US President, Washington is a land of resources. Explorers discovering the Northwest corner of this land would have been in awe of the breathtaking views of mountains, rivers, lakes, inlets and islands. They might have trembled in fear as the earth, too, trembled from volcanic eruptions. As this bountiful area was settled by early pioneers, it began to grow into one of the leading producers of commodities valued throughout the world such apples, lentils, potatoes, and grapes. During the infancy of America, word spread about this Northwestern treasure, and people began to seek this wooded paradise to make it their home. Today, Washington is home to the city of Seattle, one of the most iconic of American destinations. It is also a leading lumber producer, boasting rich lands of hemlock, cedar, ponderosa pine, Douglas fir, and spruce. Washington is a haven for deep sea catches such as salmon and halibut. The assets belonging to Washington are vast, as is the love of community that has sprung from those explorers into the hearts of its current citizens.

As the picture of the Evergreen state solidified in my mind, the idea of family traditions began to seep in. I envisioned cozy kitchens with large, country tables built from aromatic cedar filled with bowls of gorgeous apples. I imagined large pots of delicious soups, fresh fish grilled to perfection, and the warming aroma of baking bread filling every nook and cranny of a home. *Fresh Corn Chowder, Caramelized Bacon Twists, Apple Puff Pancakes,* and *Famous Ed's Bacon Macaroni & Cheese* are local favorites welcome at every meal. The deliciousness continues with *Elk Medallions with Huckleberry Sauce, Fresh Oyster Casserole, Ham and Cheese Sliders* and *Apple-*

Cranberry Bread. If a sweet tooth is something readers of this book are lucky enough to possess, they will love *Raspberry Pretzel Dessert, Katherine Hepburn Brownies, Lavender Ice Cream* and *Lentil Love Sticky Toffee Pudding,* just to name a few!

As the EAT & EXPLORE STATE COOKBOOK SERIES continues to change and grow, so does Great American Publishers. We have celebrated many amazing accomplishments since our infancy, and each new addition to our cookbook library is a testament to the hard work and dedication of our terrific staff. Brooke Craig is a glass-half full person, and this outlook keeps our eye turned in the right direction. Krista Griffin, Nichole Stewart, and Melissa Coleman continue to make sure our books are in the hands of people across the country. Christy Kent and Anita Musgrove work day in and day out to expand our content and help make our mark in the world. Diane Adams and Pam Edwards are the glue that holds it all together. Each of these women make my world a much more enjoyable place to live, and I am grateful for each of them every day.

Sheila and Roger Simmons continue to challenge me and encourage me to make strides I did not imagine possible. Cyndi Clark's continued presence is a gift. I cannot thank each of these people enough for the many things I've learned from them over the years. Having them in my life is a true blessing.

As I type these words, my 10 year old son, Michael, is sitting next to me, working his magic on his latest technological puzzle. My 9 year old son, Preston, is entertaining our family dog. My husband, Michael, will be home soon to join the fray. This is a life of family, warm meals, mistakes, laughter, love, folly and hope. Much like the cookbooks I help create, it is about the journey and not so much about the destination.

The wonderful state of Washington is the fifth state explored in the EAT & EXPLORE STATE COOKBOOK SERIES. Making it to this place has been my personal equivalent of reaching the summit of Mount Rainier. Thank you for continuing this journey with me as we take a look around…Washington.

Chris Campbell

Appetizers & Beverages

Easy Dungeness Crabmeat Dip

1 (8-ounce) package cream cheese, softened
8 ounces fresh Dungeness crabmeat, broken into pieces
1 tablespoon lemon juice
1 (8-ounce) jar cocktail sauce

Place whole block of cream cheese centered on small platter. Mix crabmeat with lemon juice. Place crabmeat on top of cream cheese, allowing some to come along the sides. Drizzle cocktail sauce along center of crabmeat. Serve with your favorite crackers.

Museum of the North Beach

Herbed Cheese Dip

2 (8-ounce) packages light cream cheese, softened
¼ cup chopped sun-dried tomatoes packed in oil, drained and patted dry
¼ cup chopped pitted kalamata olives
2 teaspoons chopped capers
2 garlic cloves, finely chopped
2 tablespoons chopped, jarred roasted red pepper, drained
2 teaspoons lemon juice
Salt and pepper to taste
¼ cup finely chopped fresh basil
Assorted vegetables for dipping such as sliced cucumbers, baby carrots,
    celery and bell pepper strips

In food processor, blend cream cheese, tomatoes, olives, capers, garlic, red pepper and lemon juice until almost smooth. Season with salt and pepper. Stir in basil. Serve with fresh vegetables for dipping.

Apple Fruit Dip

1 (8-ounce) package cream cheese, softened
½ cup brown sugar
¼ cup white sugar
1 teaspoon vanilla
½ package of toffee bits (found near chocolate chips) or crushed Heath bar

Combine cream cheese, sugars and vanilla. Add toffee bits and mix well. Enjoy with your favorite sliced Washington apples.

Megan Schoenwald, Parade Chairman
Manson Apple Blossom Festival

Ohme Gardens, Columbia River View

Veggie Dip

3 ripe avocados
2 plum tomatoes, seeded and chopped
2 tablespoons chopped red onion
¼ cup fresh lime juice
¼ teaspoon hot sauce
Salt to taste
1 red bell pepper, seeded and cut into strips
1 yellow bell pepper, seeded and cut into strips
1 orange bell pepper, seeded and cut into strips

Halve and pit avocados. Mash flesh with a fork. Stir in tomatoes, onion, lime juice, hot sauce and salt. Cover tightly and refrigerate 3 hours. Serve with bell pepper strips or your favorite vegetables or crackers.

Disappearing Dip

2 (8-ounce) packages cream cheese, softened
1 cup ranch dressing
⅓ cup hot sauce
2 (12.5-ounce) cans chicken breast
2 cups shredded Cheddar cheese

Preheat oven to 350°. Combine cream cheese, ranch dressing and hot sauce; mix till creamy. Add chicken. Bake in 8x8-inch baking dish for 15 minutes, top with shredded cheese and bake additional 10 minutes. Serve with tortilla chips or corn chips.

Gluten-Free Artichoke Dip

1 (15-ounce) can artichoke hearts
1 cup grated Parmesan cheese
¾ cup mayonnaise
1 teaspoon gluten-free Worcestershire sauce
½ teaspoon Tabasco

Chop artichoke hearts. Place into medium-size baking dish and add remaining ingredients; mix well. Heat at 350° until cheese is melted. Serve with corn chips or any gluten-free chips, crackers or breads.

J. J. Hills Fresh Grill
Icicle Village Resort

Artichoke Dip

1 cup grated Parmesan cheese
1 cup mayonnaise
½ teaspoon garlic powder
½ teaspoon pepper
½ teaspoon cayenne pepper
¼ cup chopped green onion
1 (14-ounce) can artichoke hearts, drained and chopped

Preheat oven to 350°. Combine cheese, mayonnaise, garlic powder, peppers and onion. Fold in artichokes. Pour in casserole dish and bake 20 to 25 minutes. Serve with chips or raw vegetables.

Robert Karl Cellars

Reuben Dip

4 (2-ounce) packages thinly sliced deli corned beef, finely chopped
1 (8-ounce) package cream cheese, cubed
1 (8-ounce) can sauerkraut, rinsed and drained
1 cup sour cream
1 cup shredded Swiss cheese
Rye bread or crackers

Combine corned beef, cream cheese, sauerkraut, sour cream and Swiss cheese in slow cooker. Cook on low 2 hours or until cheese is melted; stir until blended. Serve warm with bread or crackers.

Chili Con Queso

1 pound ground beef
1 onion, chopped
1 pound Velveeta cheese
1 (10-ounce) can diced tomatoes with green chilies
Corn chips
Carrots and celery for dipping

Brown ground beef with onion; drain. Cut Velveeta into cubes and melt in double boiler. Combine tomatoes and hamburger and add to melted cheese. Best served warm in a fondue pot or on low in a slow cooker. Serve with corn chips and/or veggies for dipping.

Jan Adams
Foss Waterway Seaport

Taco Dip

1 (8-ounce) carton sour cream
1 (8-ounce) package cream cheese, softened
1 (1.25-ounce) packet taco seasoning mix
1 medium onion, chopped
1 tomato, chopped
½ cup pitted black olives
1 cup shredded lettuce
1½ cups Cheddar cheese

Combine sour cream, cream cheese and taco mix in bowl. Add onion and mix well. Spread evenly in 8x8-inch pan. Top with tomato, black olives, lettuce and cheese. Serve with tortilla chips.

Shrimp Chardonnay Dip

½ pound salad shrimp, cooked and chopped
1 bottle Candelina Bianca Chardonnay
1 (8-ounce) package cream cheese, softened
2 tablespoons chopped green onion
2 tablespoons mayonnaise
Dash mustard
Dash lemon pepper

Marinate shrimp in Chardonnay 2 hours. Fold cream cheese into shrimp-Chardonnay mixture. Add green onion, mayonnaise and spices. Mix well. Add extra Chardonnay if needed. Serve with crackers and a glass of Candelina Bianca Chardonnay.

Scatter Creek Winery

Lavender Peach Chutney and Chèvre Canapés

1 cup goat cheese
1 baguette, sliced
1 cup Pelindaba's Lavender Peach Chutney
Edible blooms such as chive blossoms, violets, pansies or nasturtiums

Spread goat cheese on sliced baguette, add 1 teaspoon chutney on slice. Top with an edible bloom. The canapes can be held in the refrigerator, covered with wax paper, on trays for a few hours. Allow them to come to cool room temperature before serving.

Also try with other Pelindaba Lavender Chutneys, Mixed Berry and Hot Peach.

Pelindaba Lavender®

Peaches at Sunshine Farm Market

Creamy Green Salsa

1 (16-ounce) can tomatillos
1 (4-ounce) can diced jalapeños
½ bunch fresh cilantro, leaves only
½ chopped onion
2 cloves garlic, diced
Juice from ½ lime
¼ teaspoon salt
1 (4-ounce) package cream cheese, softened

Combine all ingredients in blender, process 20 seconds on high. Serve with favorite tortilla chips.

Jessica McKean
Dachshunds on Parade

Black Bean Salsa

2 (15-ounce) cans black beans, rinsed and drained
1 (17-ounce) package frozen whole-kernel corn, thawed
2 large tomatoes, diced
1 large avocado, peeled and diced
1 small onion, diced
¼ cup chopped fresh cilantro leaves
2 tablespoons lime juice
1 tablespoon red wine vinegar
Salt and pepper to taste

Combine all ingredients in large bowl; mix well. Refrigerate overnight. Serve with tortilla chips.

Mango Salsa

4 mangos (2 small yellow skinned
   and 2 large red/green skinned),
   peeled, pitted and diced
4 small Persian cucumbers (may
   substitute English cucumbers),
   peeled and chopped
1 green pepper, chopped
1 red onion, chopped

1 bunch fresh cilantro, minced
Juice of 1 lime
1 teaspoon garlic salt
½ teaspoon cayenne
½ teaspoon ground cumin seed
1 tablespoon white vinegar
1 tablespoon olive oil

Combine all ingredients and mix well. Refrigerate 2 hours before serving.
Will last about 36 hours in refrigerator before becoming soggy.

Backyard Wildlife Festival

Backyard Wildlife Festival

2nd Saturday in May

Tukwila
www.backyardwildlifefestival.org

Tukwila's annual Backyard Wildlife Festival teaches people of all ages to create a place for wildlife at home, school, business and other places in the community. Learn how to certify personal and community gardens as a Wildlife Habitat TM through the use of native plants, shrubs and other resources that support wildlife.

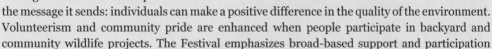

The significance of this unique event lies in the message it sends: individuals can make a positive difference in the quality of the environment. Volunteerism and community pride are enhanced when people participate in backyard and community wildlife projects. The Festival emphasizes broad-based support and participation in efforts to preserve and create wildlife habitat. Learn how habitat work can produce a cohesive effect on the community and forge cooperative partnerships among federal, state and local government agencies, conservation groups, industry, local business, schools, community organizations and private individuals.

Please visit their website for detailed event information.

Roasted Garlic Hummus

2 large whole heads of garlic
4 tablespoons olive oil, divided
1 (15-ounce) can chickpeas, rinsed
and drained

1 tablespoon lemon juice
½ teaspoon salt
2 tablespoon tahini (sesame paste)

Cut top quarter off each head of garlic and toss in 2 tablespoons olive oil. Place root side down on foil-covered baking sheet. Bake at 350° for 50 to 60 minutes. Once roasted garlic is cool enough to handle, squeeze garlic out of papery skins into food processor. Add remaining ingredients, purée in processor until completely smooth, about 1 minute. Add more olive oil if needed. Garnish with olive or sesame oil and parsley. Serve with warm pita bread cut into wedges, pita chips, or a crisp vegetable platter.

Chehalis Garlic Festival

Chehalis Garlic Fest and Craft Show

August

**SW Washington Fairgrounds • 2555 North National Avenue • Chehalis
360-748-6836 • www.chehalisgarlicfest.com**

Don't miss this celebration of everything to love about garlic! Visitors will want to explore the creative cuisine, from mild to really wild, including garlic ice cream. Talented crafters and artists from around the country bring their wares, making Chehalis Garlic Fest a true shopper's paradise. Farmers from around the northwest bring over seventy varieties of the

glorious bulb for cooking or planting. The Garlicious' ChilLounge Beer Garden offers a relaxing spot to sip on a cold Golden Garlic Beer. There is toe-tappin' live music on the stage all weekend long, wine tasting, cooking demonstrations by renowned chefs, gourmet garlic food products, antique alley, activities for children and tons of Garlicious fun!

Hummus Wraps

Hummus is made from garbanzo beans which grow in the rich soils of the Palouse. Palouse farmers grow garbanzo beans and lentils which are shipped all over the world.

Flour tortillas
Prepared hummus, any flavor
Baby spinach
Red onion, red pepper, sliced tomato, black olives, sliced radishes — use any or all of this to top your wraps

Spread hummus on tortillas. Add generous amount of baby spinach and add any other veggies you like. Roll tortillas tightly; cut into sections. Terrific for a casual get together.

Julie Hartwig, Board of directors and owner of The Shop at the Barn
Artisans at the Dahmen Barn

Tortilla Roll-Ups

1 (8-ounce) package cream cheese, softened
1 cup sour cream
1 (4-ounce) can chopped green chilies
3 tablespoons chopped green onion
2 tablespoons finely chopped red bell pepper
12 ounces sharp Cheddar cheese, grated
12 flour tortillas (14-ounce package)
1 cup salsa

Combine cream cheese, sour cream, chilies, onion, red bell pepper and Cheddar cheese. Mix thoroughly. Spread onto tortillas and roll up. Cover tightly and chill 2 hours or overnight. When ready to serve, cut each roll into ½-inch slices. Serve with salsa.

Apple Rounds

Apple (best with Gala, Fuji or Washington State apples)
Gorgonzola cheese wedge, sliced not crumbled

Slice apple into thin rounds displaying the star formation of the apple core and arrange fan-like on an appetizer tray or plate. Using a sharp knife neatly slice gorgonzola and arrange around or across apple rounds. Top off the experience with a beautiful glass of Wind Rose Cellars Dolcetto. Serves 1.

Tip: Gorgonzola frequently crumbles while attempting to slice. To deter this from happening use a very sharp, thin knife and keep a glass of water nearby to clean off the knife as you slice. The resulting presentation is well worth the effort.

Wind Rose Cellars

Brie Apricot Crostini

1 cup sliced dried apricots
¼ cup sugar
2 tablespoons butter
½ cup Riesling wine

½ teaspoon cinnamon
¼ teaspoon ground cloves
1 French baguette
10 slices Brie cheese

Preheat oven to 350°. Combine apricots, sugar and butter in saucepan. Cook over low heat. When light amber in color, add wine, cinnamon and cloves. Reduce until caramel forms. Set aside. Slice bread into rounds and place slices of Brie on top. Top Brie with apricot mixture. Bake 10 minutes or until cheese is melted. Serve warm.

Green Gables Inn

Green Gables Inn

922 Bonsella Street • Walla Walla
509-876-4373 • www.greengablesinn.com

Green Gables Inn is a historic 1909 Craftsman mansion located within the Whitman College campus. The inn is within walking distance of Main Street, shopping, fine dining, and the renowned wine tasting rooms of Walla Walla Valley. Guest visits include a full gourmet breakfast thoughtfully prepared by in-house Chef Andi. The menu changes often and every meal is prepared with the best local, fresh ingredients. Guests may also book wedding packages, or custom events, have a private chef dinner, or attend one of the special events at the Inn like the Southern Shrimp Boil. Call or visit their website for additional information or to make reservations.

Summer's Day Fruit Pizza

Crust:

½ cup butter, softened
½ cup powdered sugar
1 cup flour

Combine all ingredients; mix well. Press into pizza pan. Bake at 350° for 8 to 10 minutes.

Topping:

2 (8-ounce) packages cream cheese, softened
1 cup powdered sugar
1 cup strawberry preserves
Assorted fresh fruit, chopped and sliced

Combine cream cheese and powdered sugar. Spread on baked crust. Spread preserves over cream cheese mixture. Top with favorite fresh fruit. Cover and refrigerate 2 hours.

Fruit Pizza

Crust:

1 cup flour
1 cup butter, softened
3 (8-ounce) packages cream cheese, softened

Combine all ingredients and press onto a 12-inch pizza pan, making a lip with dough. Bake 10 to 12 minutes at 400°. Remove and cool.

Topping:

1 (8-ounce) package cream cheese, softened
1 teaspoon vanilla
½ cup sugar
2 pints strawberries, hulled and sliced
2 pears, peeled, cored and cut into chunks
2 bananas, cut into chunks
1 (11-ounce) can Mandarin oranges, drained
1 cup whole green grapes
1 (14-ounce) carton Marie's Strawberry Glaze

Cream together cream cheese, vanilla and sugar; spread over cooled crust. Combine strawberries, pears, bananas, oranges, grapes and strawberry glaze. Spread on top of cream cheese mixture. Refrigerate 1 hour before serving.

Bayside Bed & Breakfast

Ham and Cheese Sliders

½ cup butter
2 tablespoons prepared mustard
2 tablespoons poppy seeds
2 tablespoons finely chopped onion
1 teaspoon Worcestershire sauce
2 packages (7½-ounce each) small party rolls
8 ounces boiled ham, chopped
6 ounces shredded Swiss or Cheddar cheese

Melt butter in saucepan over low heat. Add mustard, poppy seeds, onion and Worcestershire sauce. Cook until onions are transparent. Without separating rolls, slice horizontally. Spread both cut sides evenly with butter mixture. Fill evenly with ham and cheese. Wrap each package tightly in foil and refrigerate until ready to bake. Bake at 375° for 15 minutes, or until thoroughly heated and cheese is melted. Cut each roll in half for perfect finger sandwiches.

Woodland Tulip Festival

Sausage Cheese Puffs

½ pound sausage
1½ cups Bisquick
2 cups shredded Cheddar cheese
6 to 7 tablespoons buttermilk

Preheat oven to 400°. In skillet, brown sausage and drain. In mixing bowl, combine biscuit mix and cheese; stir in sausage. Add buttermilk and toss with a fork until just moistened. Shape into 1½-inch balls. Place 2 inches apart on ungreased baking sheets. Bake 12 to 15 minutes or until puffed and golden brown.

Honey Chicken Wings

3 pounds chicken wings
Salt and pepper to taste
1½ cups honey
½ cup soy sauce
2 tablespoons vegetable oil
2 tablespoons ketchup
1 garlic clove, minced

Cut off and discard chicken wing tips. Cut each wing into 2 parts and sprinkle with salt and pepper; set aside. Combine remaining ingredients in bowl and mix well. Place wings in slow cooker and pour sauce evenly over wings. Cook 6 to 8 hours on low, or 2 to 3 hours on high.

Bacon Cheesecake

¾ cup dry breadcrumbs
½ cup grated Parmesan cheese
3 tablespoons butter, melted
4 (8-ounce) packages cream cheese, softened
½ cup evaporated milk
1½ cups crumbled, cooked bacon
1 cup seeded and chopped tomatoes
1 cup shredded Gruyère cheese
2 green onions, sliced
1 teaspoon freshly ground pepper
4 eggs, lightly beaten
Chopped cherry tomatoes and additional crumbled, cooked bacon for
    topping
Assorted crackers

Place greased 9-inch springform pan on double thickness of heavy-duty foil (about 18-inches square). Securely wrap foil around bottom of pan. In a small bowl, combine breadcrumbs, Parmesan cheese and butter. Press onto bottom of prepared pan. Place pan on baking sheet. Bake at 325° for 12 minutes. Cool on wire rack. In a large bowl, beat cream cheese and evaporated milk until smooth. Add bacon, tomatoes, Gruyère cheese, onions and pepper. Add eggs; beat on low speed until just combined. Pour over crust. Place springform pan in large baking pan; add 1 inch boiling water to larger pan.

Bake at 325° for 45 to 55 minutes or until center is just set and top appears dull. Remove springform pan from water bath; remove foil. Cool cheesecake on wire rack 10 minutes; loosen edges from pan with knife. Cool 1 hour longer. Refrigerate overnight.

Remove rim from pan. Serve cheesecake topped with chopped cherry tomatoes and bacon and crackers if desired.

Artisans at the Dahmen Barn

Caramelized Bacon Twists

1 pound bacon
½ cup packed brown sugar
2 teaspoons ground cinnamon

Preheat oven to 350°. Cut bacon in half, width-wise. (Cutting with cooking shears works best.) In medium bowl, combine brown sugar and cinnamon. Dip bacon strips in mixture and twist. Place on aluminum foil-lined cookie sheet. Bake 20 minutes or until crisp. Remove with spatula and let stand 5 minutes.

Arlene Hatten
Annual Holiday Tree Lighting

Weird Laws

- X-rays may not be used to fit shoes.
- No person may walk about in public if he or she has the common cold.
- People may not buy a mattress on Sunday.
- All lollipops are banned.
- It is illegal to paint polka dots on the American flag.

Party Meatballs

3 pounds ground beef
1 (12-ounce) can evaporated
  milk
1 cup rolled oats
1 cup cracker crumbs
2 eggs
½ cup chopped onion
½ teaspoon garlic powder
2 teaspoon salt
½ teaspoon pepper
2 teaspoons chili powder

Combine all ingredients and mix well. Roll into walnut-size balls. Place on lined cookie sheet and freeze until solid. Place frozen meatballs in 9x13-inch baking pan.

Sauce:

2 cups ketchup
1 cup brown sugar
½ teaspoon liquid smoke
½ tablespoon garlic powder

Combine all ingredients and mix well. Pour over meatballs and bake for 1 hour at 350°.

Cream Cheese Ball

2 (8-ounce) packages cream cheese, softened
1 (8.5-ounce) can crushed pineapple, drained
1½ cups chopped bell pepper
1 tablespoon onion powder
1 tablespoon seasoning salt
2 cups chopped nuts, divided

Whip cream cheese. Add remaining ingredients, reserving ½ cup nuts. Form into ball and roll in remaining nuts. Serve with good quality crackers.

Olive-Filled Cheese Balls

1 cup shredded sharp Cheddar cheese
2 tablespoons butter, softened
½ cup flour
Dash cayenne pepper
Olives (stuffed)

Preheat oven to 400°. Combine cheese and butter, blend well. Fold in flour and cayenne. Drop rounded spoonfuls onto baking sheet. Press olive in center and bake 15 minutes.

Sweet and Spicy Nuts

¾ cup sugar

1 tablespoon salt

1 tablespoon chili powder

2 teaspoons cinnamon

2 teaspoons cayenne pepper

1 large egg white

2 cups raw cashews

2 cups raw almonds

Preheat oven to 300°. Spray baking sheet with nonstick cooking spray. In small bowl, combine sugar, salt, chili powder, cinnamon and cayenne pepper; whisk well. In separate, large bowl, beat egg white until frothy. Add cashews, almonds and spiced sugar mixture; toss and coat well. Spread out nuts on baking sheet and bake 45 minutes, stirring once, until browned. Cool on baking sheet, stirring occasionally. Store in airtight container, will keep 2 days.

Foss Waterway Seaport is a gorgeous venue for various events.

Herb Crackers

1 cup flour
½ teaspoon baking powder
½ teaspoon dry mustard
¼ teaspoon salt
1 cup finely shredded Swiss cheese
¼ cup butter, softened
¼ cup finely chopped toasted almonds
2 tablespoons finely snipped chives
2 to 3 tablespoons milk

Combine flour, baking powder, mustard and salt; set aside. In a medium mixing bowl, beat cheese and butter with an electric mixer on medium speed until well combined. Gradually add flour mixture, beating at low speed until well mixed and crumbly. Stir in almonds and chives. Add milk, 1 tablespoon at a time, stirring until dough clings together. Form dough into square log about 8 inches long and 1½ inches square. Wrap in plastic wrap and refrigerate several hours. Cut dough into ¼-inch-thick slices. Place slices 1 inch apart on lightly greased cookie sheets. Bake at 400° for 7 to 9 minutes or until lightly browned on edges and bottom. Let stand about 1 minute on cookie sheets. Cool completely on wire racks. Can be stored in airtight container up to 3 days.

Pelindaba's Famous Lavender Lemonade

Lavender Extract:

2 cups water
3 teaspoons Pelindaba's Organic Culinary Lavender

Bring water to a boil. Add lavender, cover saucepan, and steep 30 minutes. Strain and reserve liquid.

Lemonade:

Juice of 3 lemons	**1 quart water**
½ cup sugar, or to taste	**Fresh lavender flowers for garnish**

Add 2 cups Lavender Extract, lemon juice and sugar to 1 quart water. Stir well to dissolve. Chill and serve over ice. Garnish with lavender flowers. Makes 1 quart.

Pelindaba Lavender®

Summer's Day Punch

1½ cups strawberries
3 (6-ounce) cans frozen lemonade
2 quarts ginger ale, chilled

Add strawberries and lemonade to blender. Using lemonade cans, add 3 cans water to blender. Blend well. Pour into punch bowl. Add ginger ale and ice. Sweeten with sugar if needed.

Wedding Day Champagne Punch

12 ounces frozen fruit punch, partially thawed
3 cups water
1½ cups fresh, sliced strawberries
⅔ cup orange juice
2 tablespoons lemon juice
24 ounces ginger ale
1 bottle champagne

In punch bowl, combine fruit punch, water, strawberries and juices. Stir to dissolve punch. Slowly pour in ginger ale and champagne. Add ice or ice ring.

Hot Chocolate

1 (14-ounce) can sweetened condensed milk
½ cup cocoa, unsweetened
1 ½ teaspoons vanilla extract
⅛ teaspoon salt
6½ cups hot water

In saucepan, combine condensed milk, cocoa, vanilla and salt over medium heat; mix well. Slowly add water. Heat thoroughly, stirring often. Serve hot.

Kahlúa Coffee

1 cup brewed coffee, cooled
1½ ounces Kahlúa
1 ounce half-and-half
Sugar to taste
Whipped cream
Cinnamon

Mix coffee, Kahlúa, half-and-half and sugar in tall glass or cup. Add ice cubes. Top with whipped cream and sprinkle with cinnamon.

Bread & Breakfast

New Year's Day Cornbread

1 cup flour

1 cup cornmeal

¼ cup sugar

4 teaspoons baking powder

1 teaspoon salt

1 cup milk

¼ cup vegetable oil

1 egg

Combine flour, cornmeal, sugar, baking powder and salt; mix well. In separate bowl mix milk, oil and egg until blended. Add to dry ingredients and gently stir until moist. May be lumpy. Bake in 8x8-inch square baking dish at 400° for 25 minutes or until golden brown.

Kent Cornucopia Days

Kent Cornucopia Days

Österbottens Limpa

(Limpa from Osterbothnia)

½ cup molasses
1 tablespoon grated orange peel
1 cup water
2 teaspoons caraway, fennel or anise
  seed
1 tablespoon shortening
½ teaspoon baking soda

2 cups buttermilk
1 teaspoon sugar
¼ cup warm water
1 small package yeast
3 cups rye flour
1½ teaspoon salt
3 to 3½ cups white flour

Bring molasses, orange peel, water, caraway seed and shortening to a boil. Once boiling, remove immediately from heat and stir in baking soda. Pour into large mixing bowl. Add buttermilk. Cool to lukewarm. Meanwhile, add sugar to warm water, add yeast and stir lightly. Allow it to foam slightly. Add yeast to molasses mixture; mix well. Add rye flour gradually, beating well with each addition. Add salt. Add white flour gradually, beating well. When dough is firm, let rest 15 minutes, covered with cloth and out of draft. Knead on floured board until smooth and elastic. Let rise in greased bowl 1 hour. Form into 3 balls, place in greased and floured cake pans. Press down dough with your hand, forcing it out to the edges of each pan. Let it rise another 30 minutes. Brush with lightly beaten egg white for glossy finish, or with 1 tablespoon molasses and 4 tablespoons water mixture for a soft, sweet finish. For a moister product, brush with molasses-water mixture three times: before placing in oven, once during baking and once when you take loaves out. Bake at 350° for 45 to 50 minutes. Makes 3 round, 9-inch diameter loaves.

Syrene Forsman
Nordic Heritage Museum

Hardangerlefse

2 eggs
1⅛ cups sugar
½ cup plus 1 tablespoon melted butter
2⅛ cups buttermilk
1 teaspoon baking powder
8 to 10 cups wheat flour or barley flour
Softened butter mixed with sugar and cinnamon to taste
   for spread

Mix eggs with 1⅛ cups sugar and melted butter. Stir in buttermilk. Mix baking powder with 8 cups flour and stir into sugar mixture; blend well. If dough is not easy to roll out, add additional flour till reaches this consistency. (Barley flour makes it easier to roll out.) Bake on griddle or in dry frying pan till golden brown. Spread softened butter mixture onto the lefse, roll up and cut in 1 to 1½-inch bite-size pieces.

Nordic Heritage Museum

Palouse Grains Bread

4 tablespoons lemon juice
5¾ cups water, divided
¾ cup cracked grains
¾ cup brown sugar
3 tablespoons active dry yeast
1 teaspoon sugar
½ cup oil

¼ cup molasses
3 tablespoons salt
4 cups milk
6 cups freshly ground whole-wheat bread flour*
12 cups white flour plus more for kneading

In a 1-quart saucepan, bring lemon juice and 1¾ cups water to boil. Remove from heat and add cracked grains and brown sugar. Allow to sit 15 minutes to soften grains and dissolve sugar. Heat 4 cups water to 115°. In large bread mixing bowl, dissolve yeast and sugar in water. When yeast mixture is thoroughly dissolved, add oil, molasses and salt. Add milk to grain mixture to cool, add grain mixture to yeast mixture. Gradually add freshly ground whole-wheat bread flour, and 12 cups white flour. Knead 10 minutes, adding additional flour as needed. Cover and let rise until doubled. Punch down dough and form into 6 loaves, and allow to rise until doubled. Bake at 375° to an internal temperature of 180°.

*"Cabernet" whole-wheat from the Palouse region is a good choice.

Craig and Terri Walters
Artisans at the Dahmen Barn

Palouse Grains

Craig and Terri Walters have an agriculture research business (Pacer Corp) and works with wheat breeders to develop grains for the Palouse region. Currently, favorite grains for bread are "Blanca Grande" for a white loaf, or "Cabernet" for a more traditional darker whole-wheat bread. Terri and Craig are also resident artists at Artisans at the Dahmen Barn.

Westport Winery French Bread

½ **cup milk**
1¼ **cup warm water, divided**
1 **package active dry yeast**
1½ **tablespoon butter**
4 **cups flour**
2 **tablespoons sugar**
2 **teaspoon salt**

Combine milk and ½ cup water in microwave safe bowl and heat 60 seconds. While this cools, dissolve yeast in remaining ¾ cup water. Let yeast rest 10 minutes. Add yeast to milk mixture; add butter. In separate mixing bowl combine flour, sugar and salt. Make a hole in center of dry ingredients and pour in combined liquids. Stir until mixed and cover with damp cloth. Let is rise in a warm place about 2 hours or until it doubles in size. Punch down and divide in 2 equal parts. Roll or press out each half with your fingers into a flat oblong, then roll it up to make a loaf. Place on greased cookie sheet and let rise again until double. Cut diagonal slits on top and bake 400° for 15 minutes. Reduce the temperature to 350° and bake additional 30 minutes.

Westport Winery

Rose's Bad-to-the-Bone Beer Bread

1 cup milk
½ cup honey, divided
2 cups whole-wheat flour, divided
4 cups unbleached white flour, divided
½ cup Scotch oats
2 packages active dry yeast
2 cups lentils, cooked and puréed
¾ cup beer
4 tablespoons butter
1 tablespoon salt

Warm milk and mix with 2 tablespoons honey, 1 cup each wheat and white flour, oats and yeast. Gently blend and let rest 15 to 20 minutes. In blender, mix lentils, beer, butter, salt and remaining honey until well blended. Add lentil mixture to yeast mixture. Add remaining flour, 1 cup at a time, until dough becomes moderately stiff. Turn out onto floured board and knead 5 minutes. Place in a large, warm, greased ceramic bowl. Lightly oil dough and let rise in a warm, non-drafty area for 1 hour. Dough should double in size. Punch down carefully. Turn dough out onto floured board and knead 5 minutes, adding little bits of flour to avoid sticking. Divide dough in half. Let rest 5 minutes. Knead each half 1 more minute and shape each into a rectangle. Roll into a loaf. Place greased bread pan and let rise 30 minutes. Bake 35 to 45 minutes at 375°. Lightly butter tops. Remove from pans and cool completely before cutting.

Rose Graham
National Lentil Festival

Lemon Poppy Seed Bread

1 box lemon cake mix
4 eggs
1 cup water
1 (3.4-ounce) package lemon instant pudding mix
2 tablespoons poppy seeds

Combine all ingredients and mix well. Bake in greased and floured loaf pan at 350° for 40 minutes.

Virginia Collins, Board Member
Sidney Art Gallery and Museum

Mom's Cranberry Bread

1 orange, for juice and rind
2 cups flour
1 cup sugar
½ teaspoon salt
1½ teaspoons baking powder

½ teaspoon baking soda
2 tablespoons melted shortening
1 egg, beaten
1 cup fresh cranberry halves
1 cup chopped walnuts

Preheat oven to 325°. Grease and flour 9x5-inch loaf pan. Using a grater with small holes, grate rind off orange. Squeeze orange juice into a measuring cup, and add rind and enough hot water to equal ¾ cup; set aside. Sift flour, sugar, salt, baking powder and baking soda into a medium-size mixing bowl. Combine orange juice mixture with shortening and egg, and add to dry ingredients. Mix well. Stir in berries and nuts. Pour into prepared loaf pan. Bake 45 to 60 minutes, until toothpick inserted in center comes out clean.

Apple-Cranberry Bread

1 cup vegetable oil
2 cups sugar
3 eggs
3 cups flour
1 teaspoon baking soda
½ teaspoon salt

1 teaspoon cinnamon
2 cups whole fresh cranberries
2 cups apples, peeled and chopped
2 cups pecans, chopped
1 teaspoon vanilla
Powdered sugar

Beat oil, sugar and eggs until smooth. Mix flour, baking soda, salt and cinnamon together; add to oil mixture. Dough will be stiff. Add cranberries, apples, pecans and vanilla, stirring well. Bake in greased and floured bread pans at 325° for 40 minutes, then 350° for 10 to 15 minutes until inserted toothpick comes out clean. Cool 10 minutes. Turn out and dust with powdered sugar. Makes 2 large loaves or 3 small loaves.

Manson Apple Blossom Festival

Manson Apple Blossom Festival and Parade

Second Weekend in May

Downtown Manson
509-687-3833
www.MansonAppleBlossom.com

The Manson Apple Blossom Festival started in 1921 as a parade through the orchards to check out the blossoms for the upcoming crop. Then it became a parade through town on a Saturday with Chicken Noodle Dinner. Now the Manson Apple Blossom coincides with Mother's Day weekend. Friday night the Pageant kicks off the celebration with the crowning of the Queen with the crown made long ago of shell apple blossoms. The blare of the fire siren Saturday morning alerts the thousands lining the streets that the Parade, highlighted by many local floats and unique entries, is about to begin. Each year a well deserving local resident(s) is chosen Grand Marshal to lead the parade—the best little parade around. Visit mansonappleblossom.com for activities not to be missed.

Apple Muffins

½ cup vegetable oil
1 cup sugar
1 tablespoon vanilla
½ teaspoon salt
½ teaspoon baking soda
½ teaspoon cinnamon

1½ cups flour
2 eggs
½ cup flaked coconut
1 cup peeled and chopped apples
½ cup chopped pecans

Mix all ingredients. Fill greased muffin cups two-thirds full. Bake at 350° for 25 minutes.

Pam Heinrich, Volunteer
Sidney Art Gallery and Museum

Sidney Museum and Arts Association

202 Sidney Avenue • Port Orchard
360-876-3693 • www.sidneymuseumandarts.com

The Sidney Art Gallery and Museum are located in a National and State historic site built in 1908, the first Port Orchard Masonic Hall. The Sidney Art Gallery displays original art of Pacific Northwest artists and features a unique show monthly. Upstairs, the Sidney Museum features vignettes of life in early South Kitsap County, including a general store, school, doctor's office and hardware store. The Log Cabin Museum, located up the hill at 416 Sidney Avenue, built in 1914, features changing exhibits of home life in South Kitsap during the past 100 years as well as items typically used and tells the ongoing story of the Orchards, a family of mannequins. In the picture, Mother Orchard (played by Bobbie Stewart of the Olde Central Antique Mall) is making jam and bread while Teddy, ever mischievous, helps.

Special Blueberry Muffins

2 cups flour
2 teaspoons baking powder
½ teaspoon salt
1¼ cups sugar plus more for
    sprinkling

½ cup butter, softened
2 eggs
½ cup milk
2½ cups blueberries, divided

Preheat oven to 350°. Grease muffin pan. Sift flour with baking powder and salt and set aside. In large bowl, combine 1¼ cups sugar with butter and beat until light and fluffy. Add eggs 1 at a time, beating well after each addition. Add flour mixture alternately with milk, beating by hand until just combined. With fork, mash ½ cup berries. Stir into batter with fork, add remaining whole berries, and mix gently. Fill muffin tins ¾ full. Sprinkle each with additional sugar as desired. Bake 25 to 30 minutes, or until lightly browned. Let cool in tins 15 minutes; remove, and serve warm. Makes 12 muffins.

Linda Lowber, loyal customer
Sunshine Farm Market

Bran Muffins

2 cups sugar
½ cup shortening
4 eggs
4 cups (1 quart) buttermilk
2 cups water

5 cups flour
5 teaspoons baking soda
1 (1-pound) box Kellogg's Bran
    Buds

Cream together sugar and shortening. Add eggs, 1 at a time. Add buttermilk, water, flour and baking soda; mix well. Add Bran Buds. Refrigerate at least 6 hours before baking. Do not stir mixture while chilling. Pour into greased muffin cups and bake at 400° for 20 to 25 minutes.

Kathy McKean
Dachshunds on Parade

Raisin Scones

2 sticks (1 cup) unsalted butter,
   softened
¼ cup plus 2 tablespoons sugar,
   divided
3 large eggs

3 cups all-purpose flour
1 tablespoon baking powder
⅓ cup buttermilk
½ cup raisins

Preheat oven to 350°. Using an electric mixer, beat butter until creamy.
Add ¼ cup sugar and mix well. Add eggs, 1 at a time, beating well
after each. Add flour, baking powder and buttermilk; mix well. Fold
in raisins by hand. Spoon dough into 12 mounds on a greased baking
sheet. Sprinkle with remaining sugar. Bake 20 minutes. Makes 12
scones.

Puget Sound Navy Museum

251 First Street • Bremerton
360-479-7447
www.PugetSoundNavyMuseum.org

The Puget Sound Navy Museum is a great way for
people of all ages to experience the U.S. Navy. Housed
in historic Building 50, PSNM is conveniently located
off base, next door to the ferry terminal in Bremerton, just
a scenic ferry ride from downtown Seattle. The museum is
full of fun and informative exhibits about the history of, life in,
and work of the U.S. Navy. PSNM is hands-on, family-friendly,
and admission is free.

Pacific Northwest Wild Huckleberry Breakfast Scones

3 cups flour
⅓ cup sugar
2½ teaspoons baking powder
½ teaspoon baking soda
¼ teaspoon salt
¾ cup butter

1 cup buttermilk
⅔ cup wild blue or red huckleberries
  (may substitute blueberries)
Milk
Sugar

Preheat oven to 400°. Combine flour, sugar, baking powder, baking soda, salt and butter in food processor and pulse until well combined. Add buttermilk. Pulse until combined. Turn out to lightly floured surface and gently knead in berries. Form into 2 rounds about ¾ inch thick. Brush with milk and sprinkle with sugar. Cut each circle into 8 wedges. Place on parchment covered baking sheet and bake 12 to 15 minutes until golden.

Joyce Jensen
Naval Undersea Museum

Never-Fail Breakfast Scones

2 cups flour
1 tablespoon baking powder
2 teaspoons sugar

1 teaspoon salt
1½ cups heavy cream

Preheat oven to 425°. Combine dry ingredients and mix well with fork. Slowly add cream, stirring constantly, till dough forms. (May add a bit more cream if dough is too dry.) Place dough on lightly floured board and knead 4 to 5 times. Pat dough into rectangle about 1 inch thick. Cut into 12 pieces and place on baking sheet. Bake 12 minutes until tops are lightly browned.

Streusel Topping:

2 tablespoons butter
3 tablespoons flour
2 tablespoons sugar

2 tablespoons finely chopped
almonds or walnuts

In a small bowl combine butter, flour, sugar and almonds. Blend with a fork until crumbly. Sprinkle on top of plain scones before baking and lightly press into dough.

Bayside Bed & Breakfast

Fisher Fair Scones

2½ cups Fisher Blend Flour
2 teaspoons baking powder
2 tablespoons sugar
½ tablespoon salt
6 tablespoons shortening
½ cup raisins (optional)
¾ cup milk

Sift flour. Re-sift with other dry ingredients. Work shortening into dry ingredients with fingers. Add raisins and mix thoroughly. Add milk to mixture. (If raisins are omitted, add additional 2 tablespoons milk). Turn out onto floured board and divide into 2 equal pieces. Roll or pat each into ¾-inch-thick circle. Cut into wedge-shaped pieces (like a pie) and bake 15 minutes at 450° on an ungreased baking sheet. To serve like they do at the fair: Split open but do not cut clear through and fill with butter and jam.

Washington State Fair—Do the Puyallup

Washington State Fair — Do the Puyallup

September

Washington State Fair Events Center
Puyallup
253-845-1771
www.thefair.com

One of the biggest fairs in the world lights up Washington for seventeen days each September with star-studded entertainment, the PRCA Rodeo, rides, animals, delicious food, feature exhibits, activities for the kids and much, much more. The Washington State Fair—Do the Puyallup is the largest fair in Washington state. Started in 1900 and truly a staple of an American pastime, the Washington State Fair—Do the Puyallup is a must-do on any travel list.

Cherry and White Chocolate Scones

3½ cups flour, divided
1½ tablespoons baking powder
¾ teaspoon salt
½ cup sugar

2 cups heavy cream
2 cups pitted Bing cherries, coarsely
  chopped
1 cup white chocolate chips

Preheat oven to 350°. In mixing bowl combine 3 cups flour, baking powder, salt and sugar; slowly stir in heavy cream. Toss cherries and white chocolate with remaining ½ cup flour to coat them, then fold these into the scone mixture, stirring as little as possible. Form into desired size scones and place on greased baking sheet. Brush top with a bit of additional heavy cream and then sprinkle with a little additional sugar. Bake 20 to 30 minutes; serve warm if possible. These scones freeze well, place in a zip-close bag for freshness.

The Ivy Wild • www.theivywildinn.com
Courtesy of Ohme Gardens

Mother's Day Tea at Ohme Gardens

A special afternoon in the Gardens to celebrate mothers! Dine with Ivy Wild Inn Catering as they offer fresh pastries and refreshing beverages for purchase. Michael's Photography provides special discount photo packages to savor the memories for years to come. Bring the family and enjoy a tea party in the garden this Mother's Day at Ohme Gardens. Garden hours are 9am to 6pm, tea party will carry on from 11:30am to 3:30pm. Free plant to all Mothers.

Southern Quinoa Breakfast Medley
(Gluten-free)

¼ cup diced roasted red pepper
¼ cup diced sweet onion
¼ cup corn
1 teaspoon minced garlic
1 teaspoon chili powder
1 teaspoon cumin
1 tablespoon olive oil
1 cup cooked quinoa
1 small bunch cilantro, chopped
1 egg, poached
¼ avocado, sliced
Salt and pepper to taste

Sauté red pepper, onion, corn, garlic, chili powder and cumin in saucepan with olive oil until tender. Add cooked quinoa and cilantro and cook 5 minutes. Top with poached egg and avocado. Drizzle with olive oil, salt and pepper…serve hot!

Green Gables Inn

Apple Cinnamon Sticky Buns

1 small apple, peeled, cored and
   chopped
½ cup light brown sugar
2 teaspoons cinnamon

1 teaspoon ground nutmeg
1 (10-ounce) can biscuits
⅓ cup melted butter

Preheat oven to 375°. Grease an 8-inch baking dish and spread chopped apple on bottom. Combine brown sugar, cinnamon and nutmeg in shallow bowl; mix well. Separate biscuits and coat on all sides with brown sugar mixture. Arrange biscuits over apples in baking dish. Sprinkle any remaining brown sugar over biscuits. Drizzle with butter. Bake until buns are golden brown, about 25 minutes. Serve buns apple-side up. Makes 10 buns.

Bayside Bed & Breakfast

Rømmegrøt
(Norwegian Porridge)

1 pint sour cream	**½ to 1 cup flour**
1 pint whipping cream	**2 cups hot milk**

Cook creams in heavy-bottomed pot over medium heat 20 minutes. Sift in flour, a little at a time, stirring constantly, until it thickens and leaves sides of pan and butterfat separates. As butterfat oozes out, remove to separate pan to be served later. Continue to stir and sift in as much flour as porridge can hold. Add hot milk, a tablespoon at a time, stirring constantly. Continue adding until consistency is like a heavy porridge or pudding. Whisk briskly until smooth and creamy. Serve in bowl with a depression to hold the butterfat (or pat of butter if preferred). Serve hot with sugar and cinnamon sprinkled on top.

Note: Some recipes say the butterfat must separate after flour is added. Recipes vary and it does not seem to matter. Modern commercial dairy products are homogenized and resist separation of butterfat.

Lynn Moen
Nordic Heritage Museum

Baked Orange-Pecan French Toast

This is a great make-ahead recipe. Soak the bread in an orange-flavored egg batter the night before and pop it in the oven in the morning. Easy, yet elegant!

6 eggs
⅔ cup orange juice
⅓ cup milk
3 tablespoons orange liqueur
¼ cup sugar
1 tablespoon grated orange zest
½ teaspoon vanilla

¼ teaspoon nutmeg
12 thick slices French bread
⅓ cup butter, melted
½ cup chopped pecans
Powdered sugar for garnish
Fresh fruit for garnish
Syrup

In a large bowl, beat together eggs, orange juice, milk, orange liqueur, sugar, orange zest, vanilla and nutmeg. Dip each slice of French bread in mixture, turning to coat both sides. Place soaked bread slices in a single layer on an ungreased 15x10-inch jelly-roll pan. Pour any remaining mixture over bread. Cover with plastic wrap and refrigerate overnight. Next morning: Preheat oven to 375°. Divide melted butter evenly between two 13x9-inch glass baking dishes and spread to completely cover bottom of dishes. Place soaked bread slices in a single layer in the two dishes and sprinkle with pecans. Bake on middle rack in oven 20 minutes. Do not turn slices over. If crisper French toast is desired, raise oven temperature to 400° and bake 10 minutes longer, or until crisp and golden brown. Remove from baking dishes to warm plates. Sprinkle with powdered sugar and garnish with fresh fruit. Serve with a variety of syrups.

MoonDance Inn

French Toast

4 egg whites
⅓ cup nonfat milk
½ teaspoon vanilla
½ teaspoon cinnamon

¼ teaspoon nutmeg
1 baguette, sliced at an angle into
  ½-inch thick slices
½ cup syrup

In medium bowl combine egg whites, milk, vanilla, cinnamon and nutmeg; beat until well blended. Dip bread in egg mixture, turning over once to cover both sides. Cook in nonstick skillet over medium heat until golden on both sides. Top with syrup. Serve with seasonal fruit. Makes 2 servings.

Bayside Bed & Breakfast

MoonDance Inn B&B

4737 Cable Street • Bellingham
360-647-2997 or 360-927-2599 • www.bellinghambandb.com

Nestled amid towering forests and majestic mountains, with scenic views of Lake Whatcom, the MoonDance Inn offers a relaxing escape from today's busy world. The Inn is conveniently located just minutes from downtown Bellingham, the San Juan Islands and the Inside Passage, Mount Baker recreation area, and British Columbia, Canada. Combining contemporary amenities with Old-World charm, innkeepers Gary and Linda Fuller have created an ambiance reflective of their artistic craftsmanship and European style in restoring their 1933 lakeside home. Appreciation of quality and detail clearly permeates every feature of the MoonDance Inn. Visit their website for additional details.

Mother Maggie's Boter Banket Almond Rolls
(Butter Banquet in Dutch)

Traditional Dutch Christmas favorite

Pastry:

4 cups unsifted flour
½ teaspoon salt

1 pound cold butter
1 cup ice water

Sift together flour and salt. Cut in butter, add ice water and mix as a pie crust. Divide into 8 equal parts, rolling each into 9-inch oblong shape. Refrigerate 4 hours.

Filling:

1 pound almond paste
2 cups sugar
4 eggs, beaten

4 Holland rusks, rolled into fine crumbs
2 egg whites

Combine almond paste, sugar, eggs and rusk crumbs; mix well. Roll oblong pastry parts into 4x14-inch pieces. Spoon filling evenly onto each piece. Roll up and seal at edges, moistening them with water. Cut vent into top with a knife. Brush with egg white. Bake at 400° for 20 minutes. To serve, cut each piece into smaller slices.

Lynden Pioneer Museum

Lynden Pioneer Museum

217 Front Street • Lynden
360-354-3675
www.lyndenpioneermuseum.com

The Lynden Pioneer Museum began in 1976 to celebrate the pioneer and Dutch communities of Lynden and Whatcom County. Very quickly, the museum filled up to become what it is today. The Museum has 28,000 square feet over three levels of exhibits that include a life-size farmstead with kitchen, barnyard, milking parlor, henhouse, parlor and 2 bedrooms. The Heritage Hall includes a two-third size re-creation of a block of downtown Lynden with 22 historic shops for guests to visit. The Museum also features the Washington State Center for Transportation Heritage. This large exhibit features 54 horse drawn vehicles, 4 cars, 2 motorcycles and a fire engine as well as numerous pieces of historic automobilia. The horse drawn vehicle collection is the largest West of the Mississippi and features many unique pieces such as a handsome cab, Irish courting cart, and surrey with the fringe on top.

Aebleskiver

(Denmark)

This recipe is currently served at Yulefest and Viking Days at the Nordic Heritage Museum.

4 cups flour	½ teaspoon salt
2 tablespoons sugar	8 eggs, beaten well
6 teaspoons baking powder	4½ cups buttermilk
2 teaspoons baking soda	Oil

Heat aebleskiver pan over medium-high heat. Combine flour, sugar, baking powder, baking soda and salt; mix well. Combine eggs and buttermilk, mixing well. Add dry ingredients to buttermilk mixture gradually, beating between additions. Blend until smooth. Put ½ teaspoon oil in each depression of aebleskiver pan. Fill each two-thirds full with batter. Using wooden skewer or toothpick, gently lift cooked bottom and turn uncooked batter into depression. Keeping lifting and turning out batter until all shells are set and golden brown. A toothpick inserted in center should come out clean. Serve warm and garnish with powdered sugar.

Jon Halgren and Kirsten Olsen
Nordic Heritage Museum

Apple Puff Pancake

6 eggs
1½ cups milk
1 teaspoon vanilla extract
1 cup flour
3 tablespoons sugar
½ teaspoon salt
¼ teaspoon ground cinnamon
2 tablespoons butter
2 apples, peeled, cored and sliced
3 tablespoons brown sugar

Preheat oven to 425°. In a large bowl, use an electric mixer to blend eggs, milk and vanilla. Add flour, sugar, salt and cinnamon; mix just until blended and set aside. Melt butter in 9x9-inch pan, melting in oven till bubbly but not brown. Remove from oven and arrange apple slices in bottom of pan. Pour batter over apples. Sprinkle brown sugar over top.

Bake 20 minutes or until puffed and lightly browned. Remove from oven and serve immediately.

Deanna Walter, Chelan County Assessor
Manson Apple Blossom Festival

Apple Pancake

1 large golden delicious apple
4 tablespoons butter
1 teaspoon ground cinnamon
¾ cup sugar, divided
⅓ cup flour
⅓ cup milk
½ teaspoon double-acting baking powder
⅛ teaspoon salt
4 eggs, separated

About 40 minutes before serving, peel, core and cut apple into ¼-inch slices; set aside. In 10-inch skillet over medium-low heat, melt butter (do not use margarine because it separates from sugar during cooking). Stir in cinnamon and ¼ cup sugar. Remove skillet from heat. Arrange apple slices in butter mixture, overlapping slices slightly. Return skillet to heat; cook over low heat 10 minutes or until apples are tender-crisp. Meanwhile, preheat oven to 400°. In medium bowl with fork, beat flour, milk, baking powder, salt and egg yolks until blended; set aside. In small bowl, with mixer at high speed, beat egg whites with remaining sugar until soft peaks form. Fold egg white mixture into egg yolk mixture. Spread egg mixture evenly over apple slices in skillet. Bake 10 minutes or until pancake is golden brown. Remove skillet from oven. With spatula, loosen edge of pancake from skillet. Carefully invert pancake into warm platter; serve immediately.

Bayside Bed & Breakfast

Swedish Pancakes

Traditionally in Sweden and Swedish-America, Thursday supper consists of pea soup and pancakes.

2 eggs
2½ tablespoons sugar
¼ teaspoon salt

1 cup flour
2 cups milk

Beat together eggs, sugar, and salt. Alternately add flour and milk. Let pancake batter sit at least a 30 minutes before using so flour will have a chance to absorb liquids (it can be made the night before). Heat frying pan to hot, then reduce to medium heat. Add ½ cup batter, cook 1 to 1½ minutes, flip and cook another 30 seconds or until golden brown. Pancakes are made thin. Swedish pancakes are served with strawberry or lingonberry preserves and whipped cream.

Margaret Lidberg
Nordic Heritage Museum

Nordic Heritage Museum

3014 NW 67th Street • Seattle
206-789-5707 • www.nordicmuseum.org

The Nordic Heritage Museum, located in Ballard in Northwest Seattle, shares Nordic culture with people of all ages and backgrounds by exhibiting art and objects, preserving collections, providing educational and cultural experiences, and serving as a community gathering place. The museum presents permanent collections of Nordic folk art and culture as well as features temporary exhibitions of Nordic art, craft, and design.

Each year, the Museum begins the holiday season with the all-ages event Yulefest, held the weekend before Thanksgiving. This popular Nordic Christmas tradition transforms the Museum into a sensory feast, which includes unique Nordic crafts for sale, Scandinavian music performances, and Nordic food and drink. Members and guests from near and far come to enjoy Nordic specialty treats, including open-face Scandinavian sandwiches at the Nordic Café, krumkake and lefse in the Kaffestuga, and glögg and a selection of Nordic beers in the Bodega.

Banana Pancakes

2 cups flour
2 tablespoons sugar
1½ teaspoons baking powder
½ teaspoon soda
½ teaspoon salt

2 eggs, beaten
2 cups buttermilk
2 tablespoons melted butter
2 teaspoons vanilla
1 large ripe banana, mashed

Sift together dry ingredients. Add remaining ingredients with banana last. Heat a lightly oiled griddle or frying pan over medium-high heat. Pour batter onto griddle, using ¼ cup batter for each pancake. Cook until pancakes are golden brown on each side; serve hot.

Sunday Mornin' Waffles

4 eggs, separated
1 cup powdered milk
3 cups water
3 tablespoons sugar
Dash of salt

1 teaspoon baking powder
1 teaspoon vanilla
2 tablespoons cooking oil
Flour

Combine egg yolks and powdered milk. Add water, sugar, dash of salt, baking powder, vanilla and cooking oil. Add flour for desired consistency. In a separate bowl, beat egg whites until stiff. Fold into egg mixture. Cook on nonstick waffle iron until light brown.

Serve topped with strawberries for a special touch. Serves 4.

Bayside Bed & Breakfast

Poffertjes

1 teaspoon rapid-rise yeast
1 tablespoon milk
1 cup flour
1 cup buckwheat flour
2 eggs
1 teaspoon sugar

½ teaspoon salt
1¼ cups warm milk, divided
1 tablespoon butter
Good quality butter and powdered
    sugar to serve

In a small bowl, dissolve yeast in 1 tablespoon milk. In a separate bowl, combine flour, buckwheat flour, eggs, sugar, salt and ¾ cup warm milk. Add yeast mixture to flour mixture. Whisk until smooth. Add remaining ½ cup warm milk and beat again.

Cover bowl with plastic wrap and allow to rest 1 hour. Melt butter in skillet. When it sizzles, add teaspoonfuls of batter in circular movements to create mini pancakes. Turn the poffertjes over as soon as bottom has set, using two forks. (Or prepare in poffertjes pan, if you have one.) Serve with the best quality butter you can find and sifted powdered sugar.

Holland Happening

Holland Happening

Last weekend in April

360-675-3755 • www.oakharborchamber.com

Tulips are in bloom and wooden Klompen are in style every year during Holland Happening. Located on beautiful Whidbey Island in North Puget Sound, the two-day festival, hosted each year by the Oak Harbor Chamber of Commerce, is a celebration of Whidbey Island's Dutch heritage. The festival features a grand parade on Saturday, complete with a traditional bell ringer, proclamation and street sweepers. A vendor marketplace brings crowds of people to the historic downtown area, and a Klompen Canal race for children is held on Sunday, in which small, wooden shoes decorated by children "race" down a water canal. There is entertainment of all types, from traditional Dutch ditties to performances by regional artists. Delicacies such as Poffertjes (pancake puffs) are served in abundance, along with plenty of other Dutch treats.

Puffed-Pancake Brunch Casserole

½ cup butter
2 cups original Bisquick
2 cups milk, divided
8 eggs, divided
1 cup shredded Swiss cheese
½ pound bacon, cooked and crumbled
3 cups cubed cooked ham
2 cups shredded sharp Cheddar cheese
¼ teaspoon salt
¼ teaspoon ground mustard
Dash nutmeg

Preheat oven to 375°. Spray 9x13-inch glass baking dish with nonstick cooking spray. Place butter in dish; place in oven until melted, about 10 minutes. In medium bowl, mix Bisquick, 1 cup milk, and 2 eggs with whisk until tiny lumps remain. Pour over butter in baking dish. Layer with Swiss cheese, bacon, ham and Cheddar cheese. In large bowl mix remaining milk, eggs, salt, mustard and nutmeg. Pour over casserole. Bake uncovered 35 to 40 minutes or until golden brown. Let stand 10 minutes before serving.

Bayside Bed & Breakfast

Sage Breakfast Sausage

5 pounds ground pork
1½ tablespoons salt
½ tablespoon white pepper
1 tablespoon sage
½ teaspoon ginger

½ tablespoon thyme
½ teaspoon cayenne pepper
1 tablespoon whole fennel seeds
1 cup ice cold water

Combine all ingredients together in mixer or mix by hand. This sausage is great as patties, used in a scramble dish or in gravy. Store in freezer up to 3 months.

Green Gables Inn

Breakfast Soufflé

8 slices bread, cut into 9-inch squares
8 ounces grated sharp Cheddar cheese
8 ounces grated mozzarella cheese
1 pound sausage, cooked and drained
8 eggs, beaten
3½ cups milk

Grease 9x13-inch baking dish. Spread bread on bottom and cover with cheeses and sausage. Combine eggs with milk and beat well. Pour over mixture. Cover and refrigerate overnight.

Bake at 350° for 1 to 1½ hours. Uncover last few minutes to brown lightly.

Sedro-Woolley Loggerodeo

Cheesy Sausage Breakfast Casserole

1 tablespoon vegetable oil
1 pound uncooked pork breakfast sausage, casings removed
12 large eggs
2½ cups whole milk
2 teaspoons ground mustard
1 teaspoon kosher salt
½ teaspoon freshly ground black pepper
6 ounces French or sourdough baguette, cut into ¾-inch cubes
   (about 5½ cups)
¾ cup shredded sharp Cheddar cheese
¾ cup shredded Monterey Jack cheese

Heat oil in a large frying pan over medium heat until shimmering. Brown sausage thoroughly. Remove from heat and cool 10 minutes. In large bowl, beat eggs well. Add milk, mustard, salt and pepper; whisk well. Add sausage, bread and cheeses and mix well. Pour mixture into 9x13-inch baking dish and spread evenly. Cover with plastic wrap or aluminum foil and refrigerate overnight. Heat oven to 350° and bring casserole to room temperature before baking. Bake 45 to 50 minutes or until toothpick inserted in center comes out clean.

Bayside Bed & Breakfast

Tuscan Omelet

2 medium red potatoes
4 frozen artichoke hearts, thawed and finely diced
¾ cup thinly sliced crimini mushrooms
4 plum tomatoes, seeded and finely diced
2 tablespoons thinly sliced fresh basil
4 whole eggs
8 egg whites
Ground pepper to taste
4 tablespoons grated Asiago cheese

Preheat oven to 200° and have 4 oven-proof plates ready. Place potatoes in pot with water and bring to boil over medium-high heat. Boil 20 minutes or until potatoes are tender. Drain, peel and cut into small cubes; set aside. In mixing bowl, combine artichoke hearts, mushrooms, tomatoes and basil. Spray pan with nonstick cooking spray and sauté mixture 3 to 5 minutes over medium heat until mushrooms are soft. In separate bowl lightly beat whole eggs. Add egg whites until thoroughly blended. Add pepper to taste. Spray 8-inch nonstick pan and set over medium heat. Pour in one quarter of the egg mixture. Cook 2 to 3 minutes. Lift up sides of omelet to allow uncooked egg to flow to bottom of pan. When egg is solidified, scatter one quarter of the artichoke-potato mixture down center of omelet. Sprinkle with 1 tablespoon cheese. Using a spatula, carefully fold omelet in half. Place on oven proof plate and keep warm in oven, repeating for remaining omelets.

Bayside Bed & Breakfast

Easy Breakfast Omelet

1 tablespoon olive oil
1 cup chopped sweet onion
1 tablespoon minced garlic
1 can mushrooms, stems and pieces
1 can sliced black olives

4 to 6 eggs
½ tablespoon milk
1 cup shredded sharp Cheddar
  cheese
1 sliced green onion

Heat olive oil in skillet and sauté onion and garlic. Reduce heat to low and add mushrooms and olive slices. Whip eggs with milk, add to skillet and cook to the consistency of scrambled eggs. Top with cheese and green onions. Serve with fried potato slices and toast.

Bayside Bed & Breakfast

Crystal Mountain Resort

Breakfast Pizza

1 pound bulk pork sausage
2 cups frozen loose hash browns
1½ cups Bisquick
½ cup hot water
1 cup shredded Cheddar cheese
1 cup shredded Monterey Jack cheese

Grease 12-inch pizza pan. Brown sausage with hash browns until fully cooked; drain. Combine Bisquick and hot water and mix until dough forms. Turn onto floured surface, knead till dough comes together. Press dough into pan. Add sausage mixture, then cheeses. Bake at 450° for 12 to 15 minutes.

Bayside Bed & Breakfast

Breakfast Burrito

¼ red or green bell pepper, seeded and diced
¼ zucchini, halved and diced
2 tablespoons diced onion (optional)
5 egg whites
¼ cup black or pinto beans
1 whole-wheat tortilla
1 ounce shredded mozzarella cheese
2 tablespoons salsa
Pepper to taste

Spray small skillet with nonstick cooking spray then sauté bell pepper, zucchini and onion. Cover and cook over medium heat 2 to 3 minutes. Add egg whites and scramble with vegetables and beans until cooked through, about 3 to 4 additional minutes. Spread egg and vegetable mixture in center of tortilla. Sprinkle with cheese and then roll up like a burrito. Top with salsa. Serve hot. Serve with a cup of mixed berries, if desired. Serves 1.

Bayside Bed & Breakfast

Devon Cream

1 (8-ounce) package cream cheese, softened
⅓ cup sour cream
1 tablespoon sugar

Combine all ingredients, blending well. Serve with warm biscuits or scones.

Bayside Bed & Breakfast

Clotted Cream

2 cups pasteurized heavy cream (do not use ultra-pasteurized)

Pour heavy cream into shallow glass pan or pie plate. Cover with foil and place in an oven at low temperature (180°) for 8 hours or overnight. Do not stir. Carefully remove pan, being careful not to shake. With slotted spatula, skim thick cream from the surface, leaving watery residue behind. Gently stir clotted cream and store in refrigerator. Tastes best served at room temperature.

Bayside Bed & Breakfast

Fun Fact

In 1971, a quaint coffee shop opened in Seattle called Starbucks. Since then, it has grown to be the largest coffee chain in the world.

Orange Butter

½ cup butter, softened
2 tablespoons orange marmalade.

In a small bowl, combine butter and marmalade. Beat with fork or electric mixer until blended. Serve with warm scones.

Bayside Bed & Breakfast

Good Peach Jam

3 cups diced peaches
1 (8-ounce) can crushed pineapple
6 cups sugar
1 orange, peeled and crushed
1 (10-ounce) jar maraschino cherries, drained
½ (6-ounce) bottle Certo liquid pectin

Combine peaches, pineapple, sugar and orange in saucepan and bring to boil. Boil mixture hard 10 to 12 minutes. Remove from heat and add cherries. Add Certo and stir 1 minute. Seal in hot jars.

Sedro-Woolley Loggerodeo

Soups & Salads

Quick Fresh Minestrone

2½ quarts chicken stock
1 clove garlic, chopped
¼ cup chopped parsley
8 mushrooms, sliced
1 (8¾-ounce) can garbanzo beans, drained
1 (8-ounce) can stewed tomatoes
1 (6-ounce) jar artichoke hearts, undrained

1 large tomato, chopped
3 carrots, sliced
1 onion, chopped
1 small zucchini, sliced
1 large celery heart with leaves, chopped
1 small bunch spinach, stems removed
1 cup broken vermicelli
Salt and freshly ground pepper to taste
Freshly grated Parmesan cheese

Pour chicken stock into large pot. Add garlic, parsley and all vegetables except spinach. Cover and cook over medium heat until celery and carrots are crisp-tender, about 30 minutes. Add spinach and vermicelli; cook another 10 minutes. Season with salt and pepper. Ladle into bowls, top with Parmesan, and serve immediately. Also good with pesto added in the last 10 minutes of cooking.

Linda Lowber, loyal customer
Sunshine Farm Market

Split Pea Soup

1 cup green split peas
4 cups water
1 ham hock or meaty ham bone
1 bay leaf
⅓ cup chopped onion
⅓ cup chopped celery

⅓ cup chopped carrots
½ teaspoon salt
¼ teaspoon pepper
1 small clove garlic, minced
2 tablespoon parsley flakes

Wash and drain split peas. Combine all ingredients in large pot with a tight-fitting lid. Bring to a boil, then reduce heat; simmer covered 2 hours, stirring occasionally. Remove ham hock or bone and cool slightly. Cut ham off bone and dice. Add to soup and heat thoroughly. Remove bay leaf before serving.

Tip: Split peas and lentils require no soaking.

Note: Split pea soups are very thick and may require thinning. To thin soup, heat slowly and stir in small amount of chicken stock, water, light cream or undiluted evaporated milk.

Joanne Druffel
President of Artisans at the Dahmen Barn and local farmer
Artisans at the Dahmen Barn

Yellow Pea Soup with Pork

(Ärtor Med Fläsk)

1½ cups dried yellow Swedish peas
2¼ quarts (9 cups) water
1 pound lightly salted side pork

1 onion, chopped
Thyme
Salt and pepper to taste

Clean peas and soak overnight. Cook in same water, covered, bringing quickly to boiling point. Remove shells floating on surface and add pork, onion and seasonings. Cover and let simmer slowly until pork and peas are tender, 1 to 1½ hours. Remove pork, cut in small pieces and serve with mustard.

Margret Lidberg
Nordic Heritage Museum

Sudduth New Year's Day Kansas Black-Eyed Pea Soup & Cornbread

2 cups dried black-eyed peas
2 quarts water
Ham shank
Salt and pepper to taste

Soak peas in water to cover for 2 hours; drain. In large pot, add black-eyed peas, water and ham shank; simmer 3 hours. Season with salt and pepper; simmer additional 1 hour. Add water as soup thickens. Stir frequently. Remove ham shank. Pull meat from bone and add back to soup. Serve with New Year's Day Cornbread (see page 38).

Kent Cornucopia Days

Broccoli Cheese Soup

2 tablespoons olive oil
2 tablespoons butter
1 cup finely chopped celery
1 cup finely chopped onion
2 medium potatoes, peeled and chopped
Crushed red pepper flakes to taste
Ground black pepper to taste
1 (14.5-ounce) can chicken broth
2 cups cubed ham
1 (16-ounce) jar double cheese sauce
4 cups blanched broccoli (rough chop after blanching)

In large pot, combine olive oil, butter, celery, onion, potatoes, red pepper and black pepper. Sauté over medium-high heat until soft. Add chicken broth, ham, cheese sauce and broccoli. Bring to boil, stirring constantly. Reduce heat and simmer 30 minutes.

Glenda White
Pacific Days

Fun Fact

Among the rainiest places in the world are the forests of the Olympic Peninsula. This amazing area is home to the only temperate rainforests in the continental United States, and was largely unexplored until the late 1800s.

Smoked Salmon Bisque

2 (12-ounce) cans evaporated milk
1 quart half-and-half
½ pound smoked salmon, skin and
 bones removed
2 tablespoons Old Bay seasoning

1 tablespoon Spike (vegetable
 seasoning found on spice aisle)
Salt and pepper to taste
2 tablespoons cornstarch
1 tablespoon milk

Place evaporated milk and half-and-half into a 3-quart pan with salmon and simmer for no less than 1 hour, stirring occasionally so salmon does not stick to bottom of pan (good quality smoked salmon will melt into milk). It is important to taste while cooking. After 1 hour, season with Old Bay, Spike, salt and pepper. In separate bowl, combine cornstarch and milk. Slowly pour into bisque. Stir until desired thickness. Add more cornstarch for thicker bisque or add more milk for thinner.

Kay Vallejo
MaST Center Aquarium

Marine Science and Technology Center

Saturday: 10am to 2pm • Free admission

**28203 Redondo Beach Drive South • Des Moines
206-592-4000 • www.mast.highline.edu**

iStock/thinkstock

The Marine Science and Technology Center, referred to as the MaST Center, has a number of ongoing events that seek to educate the community about Puget Sound. Water Weekend is the MaST Center's free weekly event that allows visitors and the local community to interact with the underwater inhabitants and communities of Puget Sound. Visitors can "see" and "touch" animals from Puget Sound in the 11 large flow-through seawater tanks. In addition to the amazing aquarium, regularly scheduled talks about environmental issues and a "Live Dive" program are offered that allows visitors to talk to the divers underwater and see what they see. Join them and experience Puget Sound in a whole new way.

Roasted Butternut Squash Soup

5 pounds butternut squash
¼ pound brown sugar
2 cups water
6 cups vegetable stock
¼ teaspoon minced garlic
¼ teaspoon dry onion
2 cups heavy whipping cream
¾ teaspoon salt
Sour cream

Cut squash in half and scoop out seeds and strands. Sprinkle brown sugar in a baking pan and place squash halves, cut side down, on sugar and pour in water to a depth of about ½ inch. Place pan in 350° oven for 1 hour or until squash has completely softened. Remove from heat and set aside to cool. In a large pot bring vegetable stock to a simmer and add squash meat, removing it from skin (easily done with large spoon). Add garlic and onion and simmer 5 minutes. Add cream and, using a stick blender, purée soup until very smooth and creamy. Add salt and adjust flavors with seasoning to taste. Serve warm, top each serving with a dollop of sour cream.

Note: Do not bring this soup to a hard boil, it will darken and get bitter. Simply keep it at a simmer.

Chef Erik Carlson
Teatro ZinZanni

Dutch Potato Soup

6 medium potatoes
1 tablespoon salt
1 tablespoon butter, melted
2 tablespoons flour
1 egg
2 cups milk
½ cup vinegar
12 slices bacon, fried, drained and crumbled
¼ cup parsley, chopped

Pare and cut each potato in six pieces. Cook in salted water to cover until tender; do not drain. Blend butter, flour, egg and milk. Add gradually to hot potato water. Heat again till boiling, remove from heat, and add vinegar. Serve in soup bowls and top with bacon. Garnish with parsley.

Holland Happening

Cheesy Potato Soup

⅓ cup chopped onion
3 (14.5-ounce) cans chicken broth
1 (10.75-ounce) can condensed cream of chicken soup, undiluted
¼ teaspoon pepper
1 (32-ounce) bag frozen cubed hash browned potatoes
1 (8-ounce) package cream cheese, cubed
Bacon bits

Place onion, chicken broth, cream of chicken soup and pepper in large pot. Bring just to a boil, stirring constantly. Add hash browns and cook 30 minutes on high simmer, stirring occasionally. Add cream cheese and stir until melted. Serve hot and topped with bacon bits. Delicious served with crusty bread.

Potato-Bacon Chowder with Salmon

6 cups peeled and diced potatoes
1 quart milk
1 cup diced onion
1 cup diced celery
½ cup shredded carrots
¼ teaspoon dry mustard

½ teaspoon minced garlic
½ pound lean bacon
1 pound salmon fillet
Salt and pepper to taste
Chopped green onion for garnish

Combine potatoes, milk, onion, celery, carrots, mustard and garlic in a large pot, bring to a boil and reduce heat. Cover and simmer until potatoes are tender. Remove from heat, remove half vegetable mixture; mash well. Return to pot and set aside. Brown bacon in skillet until crisp, drain and cut into small pieces; add to vegetable mixture. Cube salmon, add to vegetable mixture and return to heat. Cook on low until salmon is cooked. Season to taste with salt and pepper, and serve topped with green onion.

Sedro-Woolley Loggerodeo

Grandma's Famous Clam Chowder

1 cup diced potatoes
⅓ cup diced onion
⅓ cup diced celery
2 slices chopped bacon
2 cups water

1 teaspoon seasoned salt
2 (6.5 ounce) cans chopped clams
1 (12-ounce) can Carnation
   evaporated milk

Cook vegetables and bacon in water with seasoned salt. When vegetables are tender and water has been absorbed, add clams with liquid. Pour the "chowder base" into a 13x9-inch baking dish and chill in refrigerator. Once chilled, place chowder base in a slow cooker or double boiler with evaporated milk. Heat on low to medium 1 to 2 hours but do not boil. Note: The longer you heat the clam chowder the more the sugars in the milk will caramelize which delivers a bisque-like flavor profile.

Ocean Crest Resort, Moclips
2012 Award Winning Chowder, Professional Category
Razor Clam Festival

Razor Clam Festival & Seafood Extravaganza

3rd full weekend in March

Ocean Shores
360-289-2451 • www.oceanshores.org

An event for the whole family, the Razor Clam Festival & Seafood Extravaganza has grown to be one of the largest events on the North Beach. Local restaurants compete for the title of Best Clam Chowder on the Washington Coast and are judged by celebrity chefs. Attendees get to put in their vote by tasting all the chowders and selecting the People's Choice. In addition to the chowder competition, chefs put on their creative hats and present what they consider to be the best creative clam and seafood entrées.

The day begins with the Firemen's Breakfast of pancakes, sausage and eggs prepared and served by our local Firemen. Then, walk off that wonderful meal by visiting indoor and outdoor vendors featuring local craftsmanship, photography, jewelry, jams & jellies, teas, spices, and so much more...it grows and grows every year.

Southwest Cheesy Chowder

2 tablespoons olive oil
2 tablespoons butter
1 cup finely chopped celery
1 cup finely chopped onion
2 medium potatoes, chopped
Crushed red pepper flakes to taste
Ground black pepper to taste
1 (14.5-ounce) can chicken broth
2 cups cubed ham
1 (16-ounce) jar double cheese sauce
1 (14.5-ounce) can diced tomatoes
½ green, red, or yellow bell pepper, chopped
1 (14.75-ounce) can cream-style corn
Chopped cilantro or jalapeños for garnish

In large pot, combine olive oil, butter, celery, onion, potatoes, red pepper and black pepper. Sauté over medium-high heat until soft. Add chicken broth, ham, cheese sauce and vegetables. Bring to a boil, stirring constantly. Reduce heat and simmer 30 minutes. Garnish with cilantro or chopped jalapeños.

Glenda White
Pacific Days

Crab Corn Chowder

3 to 6 bacon slices
2 cups diced onion
2 cups diced potatoes
4 cups milk
2 bay leaves
3 (15.25-ounce) cans whole-kernel corn
1 (14.75-ounce) can cream-style corn
1 (6-ounce) can crabmeat
Salt and pepper to taste

Fry bacon until crisp; set aside. Reserve 3 tablespoons bacon grease and discard the rest. Sauté onion in bacon grease until tender. Add potatoes, milk, bay leaves and corn. Simmer 20 minutes or until potatoes are done. Remove bay leaves. Remove from heat and cool slightly. Separate half chowder and purée in blender. Return to pot. Add crabmeat and heat thoroughly. Season with salt and pepper. Garnish with crumbled bacon.

Sedro-Woolley Loggerodeo

Fresh Corn Chowder

½ pound bacon, diced
1 large onion, diced
4 carrots, peeled and diced
4 ribs of celery, diced
1 small red bell pepper, diced

4 ears fresh corn, kernels removed
  from cob
Thyme, salt and pepper to taste
Chicken broth
Milk or cream to taste

Sauté bacon in skillet until browned. Add onion, carrots, celery, bell pepper and corn kernels; sauté 15 minutes. Season with thyme, salt and pepper. Add enough chicken broth to cover vegetables. Simmer 30 minutes or until vegetables are tender. Using an immersion blender, lightly blend soup, leaving texture to vegetables. Add milk or cream to taste and bring back to simmer. Serve warm.

Stephanie Manriquez
Cascade Farmlands

Fire-Roasted Chili

2 tablespoons extra virgin olive oil

2 poblano peppers, seeded and chopped

2 pounds ground sirloin

1 medium onion, chopped

½ cup steak sauce

2 tablespoons Worcestershire sauce

1 cup beer

1 cup beef stock

1 (28-ounce) can crushed fire-roasted tomatoes

2 to 3 (15.5-ounce) cans favorite beans

Heat oil over medium heat. When oil is warm add peppers. Char 2 to 4 minutes. Add meat and onion; cook until meat is done and onion is soft. Add steak sauce, Worcestershire and beer. Cook until beer cooks off, about 3 to 4 minutes. Add beef stock and tomatoes and bring to slow boil. After 2 or 3 minutes, add beans and simmer. Cook 20 to 30 minutes. Delicious served with cornbread

Marci Ridgway
Pacific Days

Pacific Days

2nd Full Weekend in July

Pacific City Park • Pacific
www.pacificpartnerships.org

Pacific Days weekend is loads of fun for both kids and adults. The kiddos always enjoy the ever-popular children's games with the children's prize store where everything in the store is FREE! There is also a car bash for adults and supervised kids, recipe contest, the "Mutt Show" plus the big, free inflatable slides and other fun stuff. There are always lots of raffle items of all sorts, delicious food and incredible vendors from all across the state. Call or visit their website for updated information.

Wobble Your Gobble Chocolate Chili

1 pound ground turkey
2 canned chipotle peppers in adobo, chopped
1 teaspoon adobo from canned chipotle peppers
1 (29-ounce) can tomato sauce
1 (14.5-ounce) can diced tomato, drained
1 (15-ounce) can chili beans, undrained
1 (15-ounce) can kidney beans, rinsed and drained
1 cup canned sweet corn, drained
2 bell peppers, chopped
2 teaspoons Worcestershire sauce
1 teaspoon chili powder
1 teaspoon ground cumin
Salt to taste
1 (2-ounce) Dove chocolate bar, chopped (reserve a bit for garnish)
Sour cream

Brown turkey and drain. Place in slow cooker. Add remaining ingredients to slow cooker, except chocolate and sour cream. Mix well and cook on high 3 to 4 hours or low 6 to 7 hours (low provides best results). Add chocolate and mix until melted. Cook 1 additional hour on low. Serve topped with sour cream and garnish with reserved dark chocolate shavings. Serves 12.

Jessica Zielinski
2009 1st Place Winner, Savory Amateur CotBF Recipe Contest
Chocolate on the Beach Festival

Magical Mayan Salad

1st Place Winner of the 2011 Legendary Lentil Cook-Off.

Magical Mayan Dressing:

¼ cup lime juice
¼ cup canned green chilies
3 tablespoons sugar
1 tablespoon minced garlic

Salt and pepper to taste
⅓ cup canola oil
¼ cup chopped fresh cilantro
1 tablespoon chopped fresh mint

Prepare Dressing by combining lime juice, chilies, sugar and garlic in medium mixing bowl. Add salt and pepper and mix well using wire whisk. Slowly drizzle in oil, whisking constantly. When Dressing has emulsified, stir in cilantro and mint. Refrigerate.

Salad:

1 cup dried brown lentils
1 small jicama, cut into thin strips
1 (15.25-ounce) can whole-kernel
   corn, drained

½ cup diced red onion
½ cup diced red bell pepper
1 pint grape tomatoes, halved
1 avocado, cut into small cubes

Cook lentils according to package directions until tender yet firm. Drain well and cool. Place in large mixing bowl and add remaining ingredients. Add Dressing and toss gently. Place in airtight container and refrigerate 1 hour. Stir before serving.

Jane Bacher
National Lentil Festival

Lentil Salad

½ cup lentils
1½ cups water
1 teaspoon salt
1 cup cooked rice
½ cup Italian dressing
2 medium tomatoes, chopped

¼ cup chopped green pepper
¼ cup chopped red pepper
¼ cup chopped onion
¼ cup chopped celery
¼ cup sliced, pimento-stuffed green
   olives or sliced black olives

Rinse and drain lentils. Place in saucepan; add water and salt. Bring to a boil, reduce heat and simmer, covered, about 20 minutes. Do not overcook. Drain immediately. Combine with cooked rice. Pour dressing over mixture and refrigerate until chilled. Add remaining ingredients. Mix well. May garnish with parsley or place on bed of leaf lettuce to serve.

Judy Wayne, Snake River Showcase Co-op
Artisans at the Dahmen Barn

Seattle Skyline, Kenmore Air Harbor

Wheat Berry and Vegetable Salad

1 cup uncooked wheat berries
5 cups water

Place wheat and water in saucepan and bring to boil; remove from heat and let stand 1 hour. Bring back to boil, reduce heat and simmer till wheat berry is tender, between 30 to 45 minutes.

Salad:

2 cups cooked wheat berries
½ diced red pepper
½ diced green pepper
1 cup thinly sliced celery
3 green onions, sliced

1 cup frozen peas
3 sprigs parsley, chopped
1 cup coarsely chopped cashew nuts
Salt and pepper to taste

Combine all ingredients in large bowl and toss well

Dressing:

1 tablespoon Dijon mustard
½ cup white wine vinegar
1 teaspoon sugar
½ teaspoon salt

⅛ teaspoon pepper
¼ cup olive oil
¼ cup vegetable oil

Combine all ingredients, mixing well. Pour over salad before serving.

Jean Carol Davis, Friend of Artisans at the Barn
Artisans at the Dahmen Barn

Festive Roasterie Arugula Salad

This summer or deep winter salad is a pleasant surprise to all who try it. Thick balsamic vinegar is the key to this tasty salad.

1 teaspoon virgin olive oil
2 tablespoons balsamic vinegar
3 handfuls tiny arugula leaves
¼ cup pine nuts
1 cup fresh mango, strawberries, raspberries or blueberries

Combine oil and vinegar, mixing well. Toss remaining ingredients together. Pour dressing over salad and toss well.

The Vashon Island Coffee Roasterie

The Vashon Island Coffee Roasterie

19529 Vashon Highway SW • Vashon Island
206-463-9800 • www.tvicr.com

Today's worldwide coffee culture has a birthplace—the 100-year-old building that is now home to The Vashon Island Coffee Roasterie and The Minglement organic grocery. It is here that specialty coffee and fair trade pioneer, Jim Stewart, launched Seattle's Best Coffee three decades ago. Guests are invited to watch Heirloom©Coffee roasts on a vintage roaster and savor signature espresso drinks made on a hand lever espresso machine (one of only 3 in Seattle). Choose from an array of organic fare for lunch, breakfast or dinner, mouth-watering pie on "Pie Fridays" or fresh baked goods throughout the week. Guests can peruse unique offerings of over 300 custom-blended teas, bulk herbs and spices. For a pick-me-up, order one of our popular herbal and floral sparkling waters. The Minglement grocery boasts organic Island produce in season, wheat and gluten-free foods, a wide offering of supplements, and gift items.

Herbed Green Olive Salad

2 cups firmly packed pimento-stuffed green olives, drained and sliced
  crosswise
4 ribs celery, chopped
1 red bell pepper, seeded and chopped
1 small red onion, chopped
1 garlic clove, minced and mashed into paste with ¼ teaspoon salt
1 carrot, quartered lengthwise and sliced thin crosswise
3 tablespoons minced fresh parsley leaves
2 teaspoons crumbled dried oregano
¼ teaspoon dried hot red pepper flakes
2 tablespoons white wine vinegar
¼ cup olive oil

In bowl toss together olives, celery, bell pepper, onion, garlic paste,
carrot, parsley, oregano and red pepper flakes. Add vinegar and oil,
mixing thoroughly. Serve salad as addition to antipasto plate or as an
accompaniment to cheese, salami and crusty bread.

Kath McKean
Dachshunds on Parade

Strawberry Sensation Caprisi Salad

¼ cup Scatter Creek's Strawberry Sensation White Zinfandel
½ cup vegetable oil
¼ cup red wine vinegar
1 garlic clove minced
⅓ cup sugar
¼ teaspoon salt
¼ teaspoon paprika
Dash pepper
8 to 10 cups chopped lettuce
2 cups sliced strawberries
1 cup shredded Parmesan cheese

Mix wine, oil, vinegar, garlic, sugar and spices. Pour over lettuce, strawberries and Parmesan; toss. Serve with a glass of chilled Scatter Creek's Strawberry Sensation—so crisp, light, refreshing—it will be the talk of the table!!

Scatter Creek Winery

Polish Cucumber Salad

1 large cucumber (peeled if desired)
½ teaspoon salt
Pepper to taste
½ cup sour cream

1 teaspoon sugar
2¼ teaspoons lemon juice
1 tablespoon chopped dill leaves

Thinly slice cucumber. Sprinkle slices with salt and let stand 5 minutes. Lightly press excess water from cucumbers with paper towels. Sprinkle slices with pepper. Arrange slices on platter or in shallow bowl; set aside. In separate bowl, combine sour cream, sugar and lemon juice.

Pour dressing over cucumber slices. Generously sprinkle with chopped dill. Chill well before serving.

DuPont Historical Museum
Lee McDonald from Polish Classic Recipes

DuPont Historical Museum

207 Barksdale Avenue • DuPont
DuPont Museum and Visitors Center 253-964-2399
www.dupontmuseum.com • www.visitdupont.com

Located in DuPont's Historic Village, the DuPont Historical Museum is a place where visitors discover the history of Native Americans, Hudson Bay Company Fur Traders and DuPont explosive workers who once inhabited the area known today as DuPont. The museum building originally served as the village's meat market and later Town Hall and now holds user-friendly interpretive displays, artifacts and exhibits including Life in a Company Town Yesterday and Today.

The museum also serves as the city's visitor center directing newcomers to DuPont's walking trails, parks, restaurants, hotels and the Home Course golf course as well as other attractions in the Puget Sound Region.

Community events include the Annual Fourth of July Celebration at Clocktower Park and August's Heritage Days Weekend which boasts Hudson Bay Day Celebration & Salmon Bake at the 1843 Fort Nisqually site, historical reenactments, golf tournament and more!

Radicchio, Pear and Walnut Salad

1 head radicchio, very thinly sliced or shredded
¼ cup olive oil
2 tablespoons balsamic vinegar
3 to 4 tablespoons freshly squeezed orange juice, divided
Pinch of sugar
Salt and pepper to taste
¼ cup English walnuts
1 Bartlett, Bosc or Anjou pear
½ cup shaved Parmesan cheese
2 to 3 tablespoons chopped Italian parsley

Place sliced radicchio in salad or other mixing bowl. Whisk olive oil, balsamic vinegar, 2 tablespoons orange juice, sugar, salt and pepper together and pour over radicchio, toss and set aside. Place walnuts in small frying pan over medium high heat until slightly toasted, about 5 minutes. Peel and very thinly slice pear and arrange in a fan shape complimented with prepared radicchio on each individual serving plate. Garnish with walnuts, Parmesan cheese and chopped parsley. Drizzle remaining orange juice over pears and salad. Enjoy with a glass of award-winning Dolcetto from Wind Rose Cellars.

Wind Rose Cellars

Mae's Salad

1 (15-ounce) can pears, drained (reserve juice)
2 (8-ounce) package cream cheese, softened
1 (3-ounce) package orange Jell-O
1 (16-ounce) carton frozen whipped topping, thawed

Heat 1 cup reserved pear juice (add water if necessary to make 1 cup). Add Jell-O and dissolve.

Purée dissolved Jell-O, cream cheese and pears, one piece at a time, in blender.

Pour into bowl and slowly stir in whipped topping. Sets very quickly and can be easily doubled.

Sedro-Woolley Loggerodeo

Thanksgiving's Five Cup Salad

1 (8-ounce) can pineapple chunks, drained
1 (8-ounce) package sour cream
1 (7-ounce) package coconut flakes
1 (10.5-ounce) package small marshmallows
2 (6-ounce) cans Mandarin oranges, drained

In large bowl combine pineapple, sour cream, coconut flakes and marshmallows. Carefully stir in oranges. Cover with plastic wrap and refrigerator 1 hour before serving.

Museum of the North Beach

Easy Summer Berry Salad with Chocolate Dressing

1 ounce good quality dark chocolate,
   melted
¼ cup balsamic vinegar
½ cup canola oil
2 tablespoons water

Mixed greens
Fresh strawberries, sliced
Feta cheese, crumbled
Fresh blackberries
1 tablespoon chopped cacao nibs

Combine chocolate, vinegar, oil and water in blender and process well; set aside. In large bowl, combine greens, strawberries, feta cheese, blackberries and cacao nibs. Drizzle with dressing to taste and toss well. Serves 6.

Stephanie Allestad, Chocolate on the Beach Festival President and Co-Creator,
Chocolate on the Beach Festival

Fun Fact

Apples are grown and enjoyed throughout the state. A few of the varieties grown locally are Gala, Red Delicious, Fuji, Granny Smith, Honey Crisp, Cameo and Cripps Pink.

Lavender Balsamic Vinaigrette

1 teaspoon Pelindaba Lavender Honey
1½ cups balsamic vinegar
2 teaspoons dried lavender
2 tablespoons extra virgin olive oil
Salt and pepper to taste

In medium saucepan, heat honey slowly until bubbling. Add vinegar and lavender; simmer over low heat until reduced to ¾ cup, about 8 to 10 minutes. Strain and cool slightly. Whisk in oil and season with salt and pepper.

Pelindaba Lavender®

Chicken-Apple Salad Sandwich Spread

1 (12.5-ounce) can chicken, drained and flaked
½ cup apple, diced
¼ cup diced celery
½ cup chopped pecans
1 tablespoon sweet relish
Dash of onion powder
½ cup mayonnaise

Combine all ingredients and enjoy on bread, crackers or lettuce leaf as salad.

Helen Louise England, deceased, 2nd generation volunteer,
Mother, Grandmother and Great-Grandmother of Apple Blossom Royalty
Manson Apple Blossom Festival

Salmon Salad

1 pound salmon fillet, cooked and
  cooled
⅓ cup mayonnaise
⅓ cup sour cream
4 teaspoons lemon juice

1 tablespoon diced red onion
2 tablespoon chopped capers
2 tablespoon fresh dill
½ teaspoon salt
¼ teaspoon pepper

Flake salmon gently; set aside. Combine remaining ingredients; mix well.
Fold salmon into mixture. Serve on bed of salad greens or on toasted bread.

Jodee Maiorana, Resident screen printing and embroidery artisan
Artisans at the Dahmen Barn

Spring and Summer Salad

Fresh baby spinach
Avocado, sliced
Dried cranberries
Candied pecans
Balsamic vinaigrette
Crumbled Feta cheese

Combine spinach, avocado, cranberries and pecans. Toss well. Drizzle with vinaigrette and top with Feta cheese. Delicious paired with Glacier Peak Pinot Noir.

Glacier Peak Winery

Delicious Pea Salad

1 (15-ounce) can sweet peas, drained
4 hardboiled eggs, diced
3 or 4 sweet pickles, diced
¼ pound American cheese, shredded
2 tablespoons Miracle Whip salad dressing
½ small onion, diced
½ cup chopped celery

Combine all ingredients, mix well. Chill 2 hours before serving.

Vegetables & Other Side Dishes

Grandma Louie's Twice Baked Potatoes

1½ medium baking potatoes per person (not red)
Salt and pepper to taste
Half-and-half (about ¼ cup per potato)

Boil whole potatoes until tender. Drain, cool, peel and dice finely. Place in buttered casserole dish, salt and pepper to taste. Pour half-and-half over potatoes until they are just covered.

Bake at 350° until bubbly and golden brown, about 1½ hours.

Kent Cornucopia Days

Kent Cornucopia Days

July

**The Entire Kent Historical District
Centered at the corner of 2nd & Meeker Street
Kent
253-852-LION (5466) • www.kcdays.com**

Kent Cornucopia Days is South King County's largest Family Festival and is a four day Seafair event that occurs in mid-July with upwards of 300,000 people in attendance. It is the largest Street Fair in the Northwest with 600 vendors (including two food courts), the Kent Farmers Market, the largest South King County Community Parade, a full size carnival and midway, continuous entertainment, numerous educational displays, and the largest Dragon Boat Races in the Pacific Northwest. There is also a 5K/10K Fun Run/Walk, large soccer and skateboard tournaments, and several bike rides and races. There is the Lions Health Fair, Lions bingo, an art Show, a beer garden, and a wine tasting garden. Kent Cornucopia Days is another Community Service Project of the Kent Lions & Foundation, an all-volunteer organization and committee that benefits over 250 nonprofit or charitable organizations.

**Kent
Cornucopia Days**

Another Kent Lions Community Service Project

Hash Brown Casserole

1 (32-ounce) package frozen hash browns
1 to 2 cups chopped onion
2 (10.75-ounce) cans cream of chicken soup

1 pint sour cream
1 pound shredded Cheddar cheese
½ cup butter, melted
4 cups crushed corn flakes

Preheat oven to 350°. Combine hash browns, onion, chicken soup, sour cream and cheese. Spread into 9x13-inch casserole dish. In bowl, mix butter and corn flakes. Spread on top of hash brown mixture. Bake 1 hour.

Since 1974
Another Kent Lions Event

Town Square Plaza
Each Saturday, June–September
9am to 2pm
253-486-9316
www.kentfarmersmarket.com

One of Washington's oldest markets, the Kent Farmers Market is an open air market located in downtown Kent at the corner of 2nd and Smith, next to the Kent Library. Another Kent Lions Community Service Project.

Twice Baked Potatoes

6 large potatoes
¾ cup butter, softened
2 teaspoons salt
1 teaspoon pepper

1 cup heavy cream
4 tablespoons butter
1 cup shredded Cheddar cheese

Bake potatoes until soft (microwave or oven, whichever you prefer). Cut potatoes in half lengthwise and scoop pulp into bowl, being careful to keep skins intact. Set skin "bowls" aside. To pulp add ¾ cup butter, salt, pepper and cream; mix lightly. Spoon potato mixture into potato skin bowls. Dot with butter and top with cheese. Bake at 375° for 20 minutes.

White Chocolate Whipped Potatoes

3 pounds Yukon Gold potatoes, peeled
1½ ounces white chocolate chips
¾ teaspoon kosher salt
¼ teaspoon Tabasco
1½ cups heavy cream

Dice potatoes into 2-inch cubes, place in steam rack and steam until tender. Place steamed potatoes in mixing bowl and add white chocolate chips. Residual heat will melt chips as they are mixed with an electric mixer on medium speed. Add salt and Tabasco, then slowly pour in heavy cream. Continue mixing until no lumps are left and potatoes are creamy.

Jess Owen, Ocean Crest Resort Owner/Former Executive Chef
2009 1st Place Winner, Savory Professionals Recipe Contest
Chocolate on the Beach Festival

Roasted Potatoes with Herbs de Provence

6 medium baking potatoes, peeled
⅓ cup extra virgin olive oil
1 tablespoon Purple Haze Herbs de Provence
Salt to taste

Preheat oven to 400°. Cut potatoes into 1-inch wedges. Place cut potatoes into baking dish large enough to hold in single layer. Drizzle with olive oil, sprinkle with herbs and salt, then toss mixture with hands, coating evenly. Bake 45 minutes, stirring occasionally until lightly browned. Be adventurous! Mix in any or all of the following root veggies: parsnips, turnips, sweet potatoes, yams or carrots.

Purple Haze Lavender Farm

Purple Haze Lavender Farm

Kathy's Potato Casserole

2 pounds frozen hash brown potato squares
1 medium onion, chopped
1 (10.75-ounce) can cream of potato soup
1 (10.75-ounce) can cream of celery soup
12 ounces sour cream
1 cup shredded Cheddar cheese
2 cups crushed potato chips
½ cup melted butter

Spray 9x13-inch casserole dish with nonstick cooking spray. Place frozen hash browns in dish. Combine onion, soups, sour cream and cheese and spread over potatoes. Top with potato chips. Drizzle butter over chips. Bake at 350° for 30 minutes. Lightly place foil on top of casserole and cook an additional 60 minutes. The foil is important, it prevents chips from burning.

Kathy Smith
Annual Holiday Tree Lighting

Root Vegetable Smash

3 gallons water
2 pounds Yukon Gold potatoes, washed and diced into 1-inch cubes
⅓ pound parsnips, peeled and diced
⅓ pound rutabagas, peeled and diced
4 ounces (1 stick) unsalted butter
1¼ cups heavy cream
4 teaspoons garlic purée
2 teaspoons sea salt

Bring water to boil and add potatoes, parsnips, and rutabaga. Boil until all pieces are fully softened. Pour through colander and strain thoroughly. Meanwhile, in a small saucepan melt butter in cream and whisk in garlic purée. Once butter has melted and cream mixture is hot (do not boil, it will scald milk) mash together with root vegetables using a mixer or hand masher. Add salt and adjust to taste.

Chef Eric Carlson
Teatro ZinZanni

Teatro ZinZanni

Open year-round

222 Mercer Street at 3rd Avenue North
Near Seattle Center • Seattle
206-802-0015
www.dreams.zinzanni.org

Teatro ZinZanni's main event is part circus, part dinner theatre, and always magical. Described as "the Kit Kat Klub on acid" and "the hottest ticket in town" Teatro ZinZanni is a night out unlike any other. It is a 3-hour whirlwind of international cirque, comedy and cabaret artists all served up with a scrumptious multi-course feast and elegant libations.

Maris Farms

Candied Yams

6 tablespoons unsalted butter, cut into
1-inch chunks
7 medium sweet potatoes, peeled and
cut into 1-inch cubes
¾ cup packed light brown sugar
1½ teaspoons salt
½ teaspoon pepper
½ cup water

Melt butter in large pot over medium-high heat. Add sweet potatoes, brown sugar, salt, pepper and water. Reduce heat to a simmer and cover, cooking till potatoes are tender; stir occasionally. This should take about 45 minutes. Once potatoes are done, increase heat to medium-high and continue to cook 10 minutes, reducing sauce to a glaze.

Topping:

2 cups pecan halves
½ cup packed light brown sugar
1 egg white, lightly beaten

⅛ teaspoon salt
Pinch cayenne pepper
Pinch ground cumin

Combine Topping ingredients in bowl, mixing well. Pour potato mixture into 9x13-inch casserole dish and spread Topping over potatoes. Bake at 450° for 12 minutes. Serve warm.

Maris Farms

Zinful Beets

2 tablespoons butter
1 tablespoon flour
½ cup Maryhill Reserve Zinfandel
3 cups cooked, grated beets

1 teaspoon sugar
Nutmeg, cloves, salt and pepper to
taste

Melt butter in saucepan, stir in flour until paste and add Maryhill Reserve Zinfandel. Blend thoroughly. Add beets, sugar, a small grating of nutmeg, a pinch of cloves and salt and pepper to taste. Simmer over low heat until tender (add more wine if needed).

Maryhill Winery

Dutch Boeren Kool
(Farmer's Cabbage)

2 bunches green kale
1 teaspoon salt
6 medium potatoes, peeled and
   cubed

Salt and pepper to taste
¼ cup plus 1 teaspoon butter
1 smoked sausage (turkey)

Finely cut kale and place in large pot; cover with water. Add salt and bring to a boil. Boil 5 minutes and remove kale, reserving ¼ cup water; set aside. Add potatoes to pot and cover with fresh water; boil until done. Drain; add salt and pepper. Mash potatoes with ¼ cup butter and ¼ cup reserved kale water. Brown sausage in 1 teaspoon butter, remove sausage, add ¼ cup water to pan to make shuu (gravy). Cut sausage into ⅛-inch thick slices. Mix drained kale with mashed potatoes and add sausage. Add shuu (gravy) to taste when serving.

Woodland Tulip Festival

Woodland Tulip Festival
April

Holland America Bulb Farms
1066 South Pekin Road • Woodland
360-225-4512 • Toll Free: 877-7-TULIPS
www.habf.net

Woodland celebrates spring over 2 weekends with its Annual Woodland Tulip Festival. The activities include a 5K Tulip Trot run/walk, outdoor artisan and farmers market, and a variety of local vendors such as handmade garden art, jewelry, health conscious items, pet products, garden décor, art, and much more. Cute babies are all around for the Cutest Baby and Youth Photography Contests. There is delicious food, children's activities and face painting. The centerpiece of the entire festival is the Tulip Show field and display garden, where guests can stroll through the beautiful spring flowers and visit the gift shop. The gift shop is the perfect place to purchase souvenirs, bulbs, spring flower pots, and fresh cut flowers

In addition to the festival, the Tulip Fields and gift shop are open daily in the month of April 10am to 5pm. Visit the website for detailed driving directions and current information.

Sarah's Kale Chips

1 bunch kale
Olive oil
Chunky sea salt
Nutritional yeast (optional)

Preheat oven to 350°. Line cookie sheet with parchment paper. Rinse kale and let dry on towel or shake water till mostly dry. Break kale apart into slightly larger than chip-size pieces (they will shrink), making sure they're all about the same size. Remove stems. Lay out kale in one layer on cookie sheet. Lightly drizzle olive oil onto kale, making sure not to overdo it. Too much oil makes soggy kale chips!

Sprinkle with sea salt and nutritional yeast to taste. Baking times vary by oven. Check after 10 minutes and then every 2 minutes after that. Kale should be crisp to the touch. Easy to over or undercook so watch carefully. Scoop kale with spatula into bowl and lightly toss with fingers to make sure oil and seasonings are evenly distributed. Best when eaten the day they are made.

Experiment with different seasonings. Different combinations of garlic salt, herbs, chili powder, curry, etc., will yield endless flavor options.

Sarah Mathews, Assistant Manager
Sunshine Farm Market

Easy Zucchini Pie

1 cup chopped zucchini
1 cup chopped tomato
½ cup chopped onion
⅓ cup grated Parmesan cheese
⅔ cup Bisquick
¾ cup milk
2 eggs
½ teaspoon salt
¼ teaspoon pepper

Preheat oven to 400°. Lightly grease bottom and side of 9x11¼-inch pie plate. Sprinkle zucchini, tomato, onion and cheese evenly in pie plate. Combine remaining ingredients with fork until blended and pour evenly into pie plate. Bake 35 minutes or until knife inserted in center comes out clean. Cool at least 10 minutes before serving

Michelle Medina
Annual Holiday Tree Lighting

Delicious Brussels Sprouts

1 pound fresh Brussels sprouts,
  halved
Extra virgin olive oil spray
Salt to taste
¼ cup sugar

½ cup rice vinegar
Pepper to taste
1 teaspoon crushed red pepper flakes
4 garlic cloves, minced
1 lemon

Spray sprouts with extra virgin olive oil, coating evenly. Sprinkle with salt. Roast at 400° for 40 to 45 minutes, until outer leaves are crispy and nicely browned. Combine sugar, rice vinegar, pepper, red pepper flakes and garlic. Microwave until sugar is dissolved. Pour over sprouts, tossing well. Squeeze fresh lemon juice over the sprouts, toss a bit more and serve.

Olympic Game Farm

Spicy Lentil Crackle

2 cups lentils
8 cups cold tap water
½ teaspoon baking soda
4 cups oil

1 teaspoon salt
1 teaspoon cayenne pepper
1 teaspoon ground cumin
1 teaspoon ground coriander powder

Pick over lentils, rinse and set aside. Add water and baking soda to large bowl, stir to mix. Add lentils and soak at room temperature 4 to 8 hours; drain well. Add oil to medium-size heavy pot and heat over medium-high heat. When oil is hot, place one third of the lentils into a large, flat-bottomed, metal strainer. Lower strainer into hot oil. Fry 5 minutes, or until some of the lentils split slightly and are crispy. Lentils should darken slightly, but not get entirely brown. Remove strainer from oil and place lentils on paper towels to drain. Repeat this process with remaining lentils. Place lentils in large bowl and set aside. Combine salt, cayenne pepper, cumin and coriander. Add to the lentils and mix well. A marvelous topping for just about anything! Lentil Crackle is great on salad in place of croutons, as a topping for casserole instead of fried onion, or as a garnish for fruit salad.

Leni Nazare
National Lentil Festival

Lindsay Myron

National Lentil Festival

August

Pullman
800-365-6948 • 509-334-3565
www.lentilfest.com

The area of eastern Washington and northern Idaho, the Palouse, grows a third of the lentils in the United States. Since 1989, the National Lentil Festival has celebrated this wonderful little legume that is consumed by people all over the world. Each year, 350 gallons of free Lentil Chili is served out of the world's largest chili bowl, and visitors enjoy vendors, live entertainment and a microbrew tasting tent. Saturday starts off with lentil pancakes at the Lions Club pancake breakfast followed by the Tase T. Lentil Grand Parade that leads to Reaney Park. At the park is the Legendary Lentil Cook-Off, kid's activities, arts and crafts, vendors, live music and a microbrew tasting tent. Bring the whole family to enjoy music, food and fun during this two day festival. Visit the website for up-to-date information.

Country Leeks with Gewürztraminer

2 handfuls of leeks cut in ¾-inch lengths using part of the green
½ cup butter
3 tablespoons flour
½ cup Maryhill Gewürztraminer
Salt and pepper to taste
4 egg yolks, lightly beaten
½ cup Swiss cheese, grated
Breadcrumbs

Boil leeks until tender; drain and save cooking liquid. Melt butter, stir in flour until paste forms. Add wine and 1 cup cooking liquid. Cook, stirring constantly, until thickened. Season with salt and pepper. Add yolks very slowly. Add cheese and stir until smooth and creamy. Place leeks in casserole dish, cover with cheese sauce and breadcrumbs, bake in a 325° oven for 20 to 25 minutes.

Maryhill Winery

Sautéed Mushrooms

3 green onions with tops, chopped
¼ cup butter, melted
1 pound fresh mushrooms, sliced
¼ cup dry white wine
¼ teaspoon salt
¼ teaspoon pepper
⅛ teaspoon garlic powder
2 teaspoons Worcestershire sauce

Sauté green onion in butter over medium heat until tender. Stir in remaining ingredients. Cook, uncovered, over low heat 30 minutes or until mushrooms are tender.

Pacific Northwest Mushroom Festival

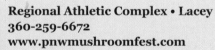

Pacific Northwest Mushroom Festival

July

iStock/thinkstock

Regional Athletic Complex • Lacey
360-259-6672
www.pnwmushroomfest.com

Each year the Pacific Northwest Mushroom Festival is held at the Regional Athletic Complex at Steilacoom & Marvin Road in Lacey. There are speakers, cooking demonstrations, entertainment, a kid's fun zone, Shroom Feast including Mushroom Ice Cream and a 5K run/walk. All proceeds from the festival go to support community projects by The Rotary Club of Hawks Prairie. Call or visit their website for more information.

Vol-a-Vent

Mushroom Filling:

¼ pound unsalted butter
½ pound crimini mushrooms, washed and coarsely chopped
½ pound button mushrooms, washed and coarsely chopped
¼ pound shiitake mushrooms, washed and coarsely chopped
½ pound green beans, cleaned, washed and cut in quarters
½ cup diced red bell pepper
1 cup diced tomatoes
4 cups washed fresh spinach
2 tablespoons fresh thyme, stemmed and washed
2 tablespoons fresh basil, stemmed and washed
1 teaspoon fresh lemon zest
1 tablespoon Worcestershire sauce
¼ pound Parmesan cheese, shredded

Place butter and mushrooms in sauté pan and sauté until mushrooms just start to soften. Add green beans, bell pepper, tomatoes, spinach, thyme, basil, lemon zest and Worcestershire sauce to mushrooms and sauté an additional 15 minutes, allowing all the flavors to blend for a bit. Add cheese to mixture and remove from heat. Divide mushroom filling evenly between 6 small, individual, oven-safe soup bowls.

To Assemble:

6 ounces puff pastry dough
2 eggs, whipped
1 pinch salt
1 pinch black pepper

Place dough over top of each bowl and seal it to the bowls' edge. Brush dough with whipped eggs and sprinkle with salt and pepper. Bake at 350° for 15 minutes or until dough has turned a rich golden brown. Remove carefully from oven and serve. Be careful, it will be hot.

Chef Erik Carlson, Executive Chef
Teatro ZinZanni

Calico Beans

4 bacon slices
½ cup chopped onion
1 tablespoon chopped garlic
1 (16-ounce) can lima beans, drained
1 (16-ounce) can pork and beans
1 (15-ounce) can red kidney beans, drained
1 (16-ounce) can black beans, drained
1 (16-ounce) can garbanzo beans, drained
½ cup brown sugar
1 teaspoon salt
1 teaspoon prepared mustard
2 tablespoons molasses
1 tablespoon vinegar
2 tablespoons ketchup
Pepper to taste

In large skillet, fry bacon with onion and garlic. Once thoroughly cooked, reduce heat, remove bacon, crumble, and return it to skillet. Add remaining ingredients and mixed thoroughly. Simmer 45 minutes.

Barbara Lourdes
Annual Holiday Tree Lighting

Baked Beans Casserole

2 (28-ounce) cans Bush Original
   baked beans
1 (15-ounce) can baby butter beans
1 (15-ounce) can light red kidney
   beans
1 pound ground beef
1 pound bacon

1 cup chopped onion
½ cup brown sugar
½ cup ketchup
1 tablespoon apple cider vinegar
1 teaspoon dry mustard
Dash garlic salt

Empty cans into slow cooker. In skillet, brown ground beef and drain. Remove beef, set aside; add bacon to skillet and cook till crispy. Crumble bacon and add to slow cooker along with ground beef and remaining ingredients. Cook 1 hour on high, 1 hour on medium, and 2 hours on low. Stir occasionally. If it looks too dry, add ½ cup water.

Joan Fogelsonger
Pacific Days

Beans and Rice

1 (16-ounce) can black beans
1 (16-ounce) can kidney beans
1 (15-ounce) can stewed tomatoes with green chilies
¼ cup barbecue sauce
½ teaspoon cumin
½ teaspoon chili powder
1 tablespoon lime juice
1 cup frozen corn kernels

Drain and rinse beans. Combine beans with tomatoes, barbecue sauce, cumin, chili powder and lime juice in medium saucepan over medium-high heat. Bring to boil, reduce heat to simmer and cook uncovered 5 minutes. Add corn and cook additional 5 minutes. Serve over rice.

Curry Broccoli & Rice

2 (10-ounce) packages frozen broccoli florets
3 cups cooked rice
1 (10.75-ounce) can cream of chicken soup (undiluted)
1 (10.75-ounce) can cream of mushroom soup (undiluted)
1 cup mayonnaise
1 teaspoon lemon juice
1 teaspoon curry powder
Panko breadcrumbs

Preheat oven to 350°. Cook and drain broccoli. In a large bowl, toss with cooked rice. Add all other ingredients except breadcrumbs and mix thoroughly. Pour mixture into 9x13-inch pan. Sprinkle breadcrumbs on top and bake 30 minutes or until bubbly and hot.

Vickie Glastetter
Foss Waterway Seaport

Roasted Cauliflower with Garlic

1 head cauliflower, separated into florets
3 tablespoons olive oil
Salt and pepper to taste
2 tablespoons garlic, chopped fine
½ cup grated Parmesan cheese

In a large bowl, combine florets, olive oil, salt, pepper and garlic. Toss well. Place in large, greased casserole dish. Bake at 450° for 25 minutes, stirring half way through. Top with Parmesan cheese, return to oven 10 minutes. Serve immediately.

Chehalis Garlic Fest

Garden No-Crust Quiche

3 tablespoons extra virgin olive oil
1 eggplant, cut into cubes
½ sweet onion, finely chopped
3 garlic cloves, minced
1 medium zucchini, halved and sliced
4 Roma tomatoes, chopped
1 teaspoon dried oregano
Salt and pepper to taste
3 eggs
8 ounces shredded mozzarella, divided
½ cup grated Parmesan

Preheat oven to 375°. Heat oil in large skillet. Cook eggplant and onion until tender, about 10 minutes. Stir in garlic, zucchini, tomatoes, oregano, salt and pepper. Cook over medium heat 20 minutes or until liquid evaporates, stirring often. Cool slightly when done. Beat eggs and stir into vegetable mixture along with half the mozzarella. Spoon into greased 9-inch glass pie plate. Top with remaining mozzarella and Parmesan. Bake 25 minutes until golden. Let rest 10 minutes before slicing and serving.

Spinach and Feta Quesadillas

1 tablespoon olive oil
½ small onion, finely chopped
1 (10-ounce) package frozen spinach, thawed and squeezed dry
6 ounces feta, crumbled
¼ cup black olives, pitted and chopped
4 (10-inch) flour tortillas

Warm oil in skillet over medium-high heat. Add onion and cook, stirring, until softened, about 3 minutes. Stir in spinach and cook 2 to 3 minutes, stirring constantly. Transfer to bowl and add cheese and olives. Spread one quarter of the mixture over half of each tortilla. Fold to cover; press lightly to seal. Place a large skillet over medium-high heat. Cook quesadillas 1 at a time in skillet, turning once, until golden on both sides and cheese is melted. Serve immediately.

Connecting Seattle and Medina is the largest floating bridge in the world. The Governor Albert D. Rosellini Bridge-Evergreen Point is 4,750 meters long and crosses Lake Washington.

White Chocolate Risotto

3 tablespoons butter
½ portobello mushroom, sliced
2 cups Arborio rice
1 clove garlic, minced
2 tablespoons sugar
1 cup chicken broth
1½ to 2 cups milk
½ cup white chocolate (grated or chips; reserving 1 tablespoon for garnish)

Melt butter in heavy-bottomed saucepan. Sauté mushrooms until tender. Add rice and garlic; sauté 1 minute. Add sugar and chicken broth. Cook, stirring constantly, until most of the broth has been absorbed. Add 1 cup milk; cook, stirring constantly, until most of it is absorbed. Continue adding remaining milk in small portions, stirring and waiting for the liquid to be absorbed between each addition. When rice is nearly finished (a rice pudding consistency), add white chocolate and stir until completely melted and combined. Once white chocolate has melted, do NOT put it back on heat. Serve immediately, with a garnish of white chocolate

Former Executive Chef, John Bass,
2011 1st Place Winner, Savory Professionals CotBF Recipe Contest
Pacific Beach Resort & Conference Center
Chocolate on the Beach Festival

Spinach and Artichoke Baked Pasta

1 tablespoon extra virgin olive oil
1 large sweet onion, finely chopped
6 garlic cloves, minced
Salt and pepper to taste
1 (7-ounce) jar julienne cut sun-dried tomatoes, drained
1 pound multi-grain penne pasta, cooked
1 cup sour cream
1 (8-ounce) package cream cheese, softened
1 cup grated Parmesan cheese
1 (10-ounce) package frozen spinach, thawed and squeezed
1 (14-ounce) can quartered artichoke hearts, drained and chopped
1 cup shredded mozzarella

Heat oil in large skillet over medium heat. Cook onion until tender. Add garlic, salt, pepper and sun-dried tomatoes and cook 1 minute. Remove from heat, toss with pasta and set aside. Combine sour cream, cream cheese and Parmesan. Add to pasta. Stir in spinach and artichokes. Fold in mozzarella. Pour into 9x13-inch glass baking dish. Bake at 350° for 20 to 25 minutes.

Veggie Pasta

½ pound rigatoni
1 (10-ounce) bag fresh spinach
¾ cup ricotta cheese
3 tablespoons milk
¼ teaspoon garlic powder
Salt and pepper to taste
Extra virgin olive oil
Freshly grated Parmesan cheese for garnish

Cook pasta according to package directions. Drain pasta well and then return it to pot over low heat. Add spinach, stirring to combine, then add ricotta cheese and milk. Stir well to break up ricotta and blend. Add garlic powder, salt and pepper. Once spinach has wilted and ricotta cheese is well incorporated, drizzle with a bit of olive oil and top with grated Parmesan. Serve immediately.

Ravioli Lasagna

1¼ cups marinara sauce, divided
1 (20-ounce) package refrigerated cheese ravioli
1 (10-ounce) box frozen chopped spinach, thawed and squeezed dry
8 ounces shredded mozzarella cheese
¼ cup grated Parmesan cheese

Preheat oven to 375°. Lightly grease an 8-inch square baking dish. Spoon ¼ cup marinara sauce over bottom of dish. Cover with half the ravioli. Spread ½ cup marinara sauce over ravioli. Spread spinach and half the mozzarella. Repeat with remaining ravioli, marinara and mozzarella. Sprinkle top with Parmesan. Cover dish with foil and bake 30 minutes. Remove foil and bake until bubbling, about 10 minutes longer. Let cool 5 minutes before serving.

Sunshine Farm Market

Shiitake-Yam Fettuccine

1 (16-ounce) package fettuccine noodles
2 cups shiitake mushrooms (fresh or frozen)
1 tablespoon olive oil
½ medium leek, sliced
1 yam, peeled and shredded
1 (25-ounce) jar spaghetti sauce
1 cup shredded Parmesan cheese
Finely chopped fresh basil

Prepare fettuccine according to package directions. Sauté mushrooms in olive oil on high until dry (very important). Remove mushrooms and set aside. In same pan, sauté leek on low heat until clear. Add shredded yams. Sauté 2 minutes over high heat. Add mushrooms and spaghetti sauce to pan and stir in Parmesan. Simmer 10 minutes.

Serve fettuccine topped with sauce and garnish with fresh cut basil and additional Parmesan.

The Vashon Island Coffee Roasterie

Barbara's Heart-Healthy Spaghetti

3 cups garden rotini pasta
5 Artisan Fresh Spinach & Asiago Cheese Chicken Sausages
1 tablespoon olive oil
½ cup chopped onion
Salt and pepper to taste
1 jar Progresso 100% Italian Heart Smart Healthy Traditional Sauce
½ bay leaf, crushed
Tone's Garlic Romano seasoning
Shredded Parmesan cheese

Prepare pasta according to package directions; set aside. Remove sausages from casings. Brown sausages in olive oil with chopped onion and season with salt and pepper. Reduce heat to simmer; add sauce and bay leaf. Add cooked pasta to sauce. Season to taste with Tone's Garlic Romano seasoning and Parmesan cheese.

Barbara Lourdes
Annual Holiday Tree Lighting

Popeye Spaghetti

1 (12-ounce) package spaghetti, cooked and drained
1 (12-ounce) package frozen, chopped spinach, thawed and drained
1 (10.75-ounce) can cheddar cheese soup
1 pint sour cream
5 tablespoons chopped onion
1 stick butter
Salt and pepper to taste

Combine all ingredients in slow cooker; cover and cook on low for 5 hours.

Maxine Spillinger, Volunteer
Sidney Art Gallery and Museum

Spaghetti with Fresh Vegetable Sauce

2 tablespoons olive oil
1 medium onion, chopped
1 garlic clove, minced
1 teaspoon dried basil
1 teaspoon dried oregano
1 small zucchini, thinly sliced
4 ounces mushrooms, thinly sliced
1 green pepper, diced
2 tomatoes, peeled and chopped
1 (6-ounce) can tomato paste
1 teaspoon sugar
1 (10-ounce) package spaghetti
Parmesan cheese

Heat oil in heavy skillet. Add onion, garlic, basil and oregano. Stir until onion softens, about 5 minutes. Add zucchini, mushrooms and green pepper. Reduce heat and cook 8 to 10 minutes. Add tomatoes, paste and sugar. Bring to a boil while stirring constantly. Reduce heat and simmer 30 to 35 minutes. Meanwhile, cook spaghetti; drain well and top with sauce. Sprinkle with freshly grated Parmesan cheese.

Famous Ed's Bacon Macaroni and Cheese

Alfredo sauce

½ cup marinara sauce

3 ounces premade meatballs, chopped*

3 ounces sausage, chopped*

4 tablespoons bacon bits

1 cup grated Parmesan cheese

9 ounces penne pasta, cooked

1 cup grated Cheddar cheese

½ cup breadcrumbs

4 slices provolone cheese

Cover sauté pan with enough alfredo sauce to cover base of pan. Place marinara, meatballs, sausage, bacon bits, Parmesan and pasta in pan. Cook over medium-high heat, stirring constantly until sauce is a pinkish/orange color. Add to casserole dish and sprinkle with Cheddar cheese and top with breadcrumbs. Place provolone in center, side-by-side, and bake at 450° till cheese is just browned. Serve warm.

*We prefer buying our meat products from Sonnenberg Market.

Mark Starr, owner Famous Ed's Restaurant
and Bloomsday Board member
Lilac Bloomsday Run

Jeff Ferguson

Lilac Bloomsday Run

Gluten-Free Fresh Grill Quinoa

½ cup diced onion
½ cup diced celery
½ cup diced summer squash or
   zucchini
½ cup diced red pepper
¼ cup grated carrot

1 cup roasted corn kernels
¼ cup olive oil
Seasoned salt
¼ cup white wine
4 cups cooked quinoa

Sauté vegetables in olive oil for 2 to 5 minutes. Add wine and seasoned salt. Mix with quinoa and enjoy.

J. J. Hills Fresh Grill
Icicle Village Resort

Herbed Quinoa

1 cup uncooked quinoa
1 tablespoon butter
2 cups vegetable broth
1 small onion, finely chopped
2 teaspoons chopped garlic

2 tablespoons chopped fresh parsley
½ tablespoon chopped fresh thyme
¼ teaspoon salt
1 dash fresh lemon juice (optional)

Rinse quinoa well till water runs clear; set aside. Melt butter in saucepan over medium heat. Add quinoa and sauté until lightly browned, about 5 minutes. Stir in broth and bring boil. Reduce heat and cover, simmering 15 minutes or until quinoa is tender. Place quinoa in a bowl and toss with onion, garlic, parsley, thyme and salt. Sprinkle with lemon juice; serve warm.

Baked Pineapple

3 eggs, separated
¾ cup sugar
1 (20-ounce) can crushed pineapple
1 cup bread cubes
1 cup slivered almonds

Blend egg yolks and sugar. Stir in pineapple and bread cubes. Beat egg whites until stiff; fold into mixture. Pour into greased casserole dish. Bake 40 minutes at 350°.

Annual Cherry Festival

4th of July Weekend

Washington Fruit Place

Each year Washington Fruit Place celebrates the Nation's birthday with hayrides, pit spitting and pie eating contests, fresh chocolate dipped cherries and a whole lot more! For specific dates and times please visit their website.

Baked Apples

2 tablespoons butter, melted
2 tablespoons brown sugar
2 tablespoons flour
4 tablespoons quick-cooking oats
Cinnamon

2 large apples, halved, cored and
  seeded
Whipped cream or vanilla ice
  cream

Preheat oven to 350°. In a small bowl combine butter, brown sugar, flour, oats and a pinch of cinnamon. Spoon onto apple halves and sprinkle with cinnamon. Place on cookie sheet and bake 30 minutes. Serve warm topped with whipped cream or vanilla ice cream.

Washington Fruit Place

Sweet Chunk Pickles

6 to 8 cucumbers, best with Sunshine Farm Market cucumbers
1 quart vinegar
8 cups sugar
3½ tablespoons pickling spice
2 tablespoons salt

Cover whole cucumbers with boiling water. Let stand 24 hours. Drain. Repeat 4 times.

Slice in thick slices. Combine vinegar, sugar, pickling spice and salt. Heat to boiling and pour over pickles. Let stand 24 hours. Pour off syrup into saucepan, heat to boiling and pour again over pickles. Let stand 24 hours. Repeat 4 times. While syrup is heating for the final time, heat jars by filling with hot water and bring jar lids (not the rings) to slow boil. While pickles are still hot, pour hot water from jars, immediately fill to almost full with pickles and juice. Immediately cover with a lid from the boiling water (using tongs or heat-proof gloves as the lids will be hot). Tighten ring on jar using a towel or heat-proof gloves. Allow jar to cool on counter then store in a cool dry place until ready to serve.

Anne Brooks, loyal customer
Sunshine Farm Market

Meat & Seafood

Chicken Marsala

¼ cup flour
½ teaspoon garlic salt
¼ teaspoon pepper
½ teaspoon oregano
2 chicken breasts
4 tablespoons butter

4 tablespoons olive oil
½ cup Marsala wine
¼ cup cooking sherry
¼ cup chicken stock
1 cup sliced fresh mushrooms

Combine flour, garlic salt, pepper and oregano. Dredge chicken breasts in flour mixture. Melt butter and olive oil in skillet and brown coated chicken on both sides. Remove chicken and set aside. Combine Marsala wine, sherry and chicken broth with butter mixture left in skillet. Add mushrooms to skillet and sauté. When mushrooms are halfway cooked, place chicken in skillet and simmer 3 to 5 minutes on each side till chicken is done and has created its own gravy. At Apple Cup Café it is served with mashed potatoes and grilled veggies.

Apple Cup Café

Apple Cup Café

804 East Woodin Avenue • Chelan
509-682-2933

Opening its doors in 1957, the Apple Cup Café is family owned and is the restaurant "where the locals eat" in Chelan. The restaurant has a Mom and Pop feel that is born from a great atmosphere and family friendly environment. Daily specials, good old home cooking and breakfast served all day are their specialties. Seating is done on a first come, first served basis and is always worth the wait. Give them a call to learn what's being served daily.

Walnut-Crusted Lavender Chicken

3 pounds boneless, skinless chicken breasts
3 teaspoons cardamom pods
2 teaspoons toasted cumin seed
3 tablespoons Pelindaba's Organic Culinary Lavender
2 cups plain low-fat yogurt
Juice of 1 lemon
2 teaspoons minced garlic
2 teaspoons fresh grated ginger
Pinch of cayenne
1 cup breadcrumbs
½ cup ground walnuts
4 tablespoons flour
Salt and pepper to taste
Oil and butter for cooking

Cut chicken breasts into 3 pieces. Pound lightly with meat mallet forming even 2-inch-wide cutlets. Pulse cardamom and cumin in coffee grinder until finely ground and uniform. Add lavender and pulse briefly. Combine lavender mixture with yogurt, lemon juice, garlic, ginger and cayenne. Add chicken and coat thoroughly. Combine breadcrumbs, walnuts, and flour. Season chicken with salt and pepper, and dredge through walnut mixture. Sauté in oil and butter over medium heat until golden brown.

Pelindaba Lavender®

Herbs de Provence Chicken

1 tablespoon Purple Haze Herbs de Provence
4 teaspoons fresh lemon juice
8 teaspoons extra virgin olive oil
2 cloves garlic
½ teaspoon Tabasco sauce
1 teaspoon sea salt
4 chicken breasts

Combine herbs, lemon juice, olive oil, garlic, Tabasco and sea salt. Pour over chicken and marinate 2 hours. Grill until tender, basting frequently with marinade.

Purple Haze Lavender Farm

Purple Haze Lavender Farm

127 West Washington St • Sequim
888-852-6560 • www.purplehazelavender.com

Purple Haze Lavender is a 12-acre certified organic lavender farm with over 15,000 plants located in the Dungeness Valley of Washington's Olympic Peninsula. The farm has incorporated the beauty and design of its lavender fields into a landscape of gardens, orchards, ponds, wetlands and buildings. The formality of the "rows of purple" is framed by a valley of open space, and vistas of the Olympic Mountains.

The owners deeply committed to preserving the agricultural heritage of the Dungeness Valley, and believe Purple Haze Lavender Farm should celebrate all that the acreage can provide: a sustainable perennial crop of organic flowers, a working farm that harvests the lavender by hand, a full line of both culinary and body care lavender products, and a tourist destination that includes farmhouse vacation rental that gives visitors a connection to America's agricultural roots.

Stove Top Chicken Casserole

2 (6-ounce) packages Stove Top Stuffing
1 whole chicken, boiled, deboned and cubed
1 cup chopped celery
¼ cup diced pimento
1 cup sliced mushrooms
¼ cup chopped green onions
1 (8-ounce) can sliced water chestnuts
1 cup mayonnaise
Salt and pepper to taste
2 eggs
1½ cup milk
1 cup shredded Cheddar cheese

Prepare stuffing according to package directions. Place half the stuffing into greased 9x13-inch baking pan.

In medium bowl, combine chicken, celery, pimento, mushrooms, green onions, water chestnuts, mayonnaise, salt and pepper; mix well. Spread on top of stuffing. Spread remaining stuffing on top of chicken mixture. In separate bowl, combine eggs and milk, beating well. Pour over stuffing. Refrigerate overnight. Remove from refrigerator 1 hour before baking. Bake at 350° for 30 minutes. Top with cheese and bake 10 additional minutes.

Jean Whitham
Dachshunds on Parade

Lentil-Turkey Spaghetti Sauce

½ cup olive or peanut oil, divided
1 pound ground turkey, divided
2 cloves garlic, minced
1 medium yellow onion, diced
1 tablespoon dried Italian herbs
½ teaspoon crushed dried thyme
1 teaspoon freshly ground black pepper
1 cup finely diced celery
1 cup shredded carrots
1 cup chicken broth (adults may substitute ½ cup whiskey)
2 cups lentils, cooked al dente
2 (12-ounce) cans chopped tomatoes with juice

In heavy-duty saucepan heat ¼ cup oil on high. Add half of the turkey
and brown, stirring occasionally. Remove from pan, keep warm and
repeat with remaining ¼ cup oil and turkey. When meat is almost done
add garlic and onion and brown lightly, adding more oil if needed; add
first half turkey and combine well. Stir in herbs and celery; mix well. Stir
in carrots. Sprinkle with chicken broth or whiskey and toss gently. Add
lentils and stir well. Pour in tomatoes, transfer to slow cooker, add some
hot water if it seems a little dry. Liquid should not be higher than solids.
Cook on high 3 to 4 hours or 6 to 8 hours on low. On stove top, simmer
covered for 2 hours on medium heat and stir frequently. Serve over pasta
and top with shredded Parmesan cheese with a green salad on the side.

Artisans at the Dahmen Barn

Rib-Eye with Demi Gastrique

½ bottle Pinot Noirvana from
   Westport Winery
2 cups beef stock

1 tablespoon butter
Salt and pepper
1 prime-cut rib-eye

Pour wine into saucepan over medium-high heat. Continue to cook until wine is reduced to 1 cup. Add beef stock and continue to cook until it is reduced to 2 cups, making a nice sauce. Add butter, salt and pepper. Stir until completely incorporated into sauce. Serve on your favorite prime-cut rib-eye, cooked to taste.

Kim Roberts
Westport Winery

Westport Winery and Vineyards By-the-Sea

**1 South Arbor Road • Aberdeen
Halfway between Aberdeen and Westport
360-648-2224
www.WestportWinery.com**

Westport Winery and Vineyards By-the-Sea was named the 2011 Washington Winery to Watch by Wine Press Northwest and voted 2012 Best Wine Tour.

Guests are welcomed daily to sample the winery's 33 award-winning red, white, and fruit wines. The gift shop is known for its incredible selection and the restaurant and bakery are open for lunch daily and for dinner on weekends. The sculpture garden features original art by local artists commemorating each of the winery's labels. Guests can explore the grape maze, toss horseshoes, play outdoor chess, or putt two greens while touring. The winery is known for its commitment to the community by donating a portion of the proceeds from each wine to local charities. The 66.5-acre farm is certified salmon safe.

Look for the 40-foot lighthouse on Highway 105 to find friends, food, fun, and incredible wine.

Heart-Shaped Beef Wellington with Chocolate Sauce

Some say this is called Beef Wellington because it was the Duke of Wellington's favorite meal, and others claim it resembled the boots that he wore. A hint of chocolate for her, a hunk of red meat for him – now there's a recipe for romance.

Beef Wellington:

1 (3½-pound) fillet of beef tied with thin sheets of larding fat, at room temperature

¾ pound mushrooms, chopped fine

2½ tablespoons unsalted butter

3 tablespoons thyme

Salt and pepper to taste

1 (8-ounce) package sliced prosciutto

½ pound pâté de foie gras (available at specialty foods shops), at room temperature

1 pound puff pastry, thawed if frozen (plus additional for garnish, if desired)

1 egg, separated

Watercress for garnish, if desired

In a roasting pan, roast beef in middle of a preheated 400° oven for 25 to 30 minutes, or until thermometer registers 120°. Let the fillet cool completely; discard larding fat and strings. Skim fat from pan juices; reserve pan juices.

In a heavy skillet, cook mushrooms in butter with thyme over moderately low heat, stirring, until all liquid they give off is evaporated and mixture is dry. Season with salt and pepper; cool completely. Spread each prosciutto slice evenly with pâté covering top and sides. Spread mushrooms evenly over pâté. Cover entire fillet with prosciutto mixture.

On a floured surface, roll puff pastry into a rectangle about 20x12 inches, or large enough to enclose fillet completely and form into a heart. Beat egg white and set aside to brush over dough. Beat egg yolk with 1 teaspoon water to make an egg wash. Invert coated fillet carefully in middle of dough. Fold up long sides of dough to enclose fillet, brushing edges of dough with egg white to seal them. Fold ends of dough over fillet, sealing with remaining egg white. Transfer fillet, seam side down, to a jelly-roll pan or shallow roasting pan and brush with egg wash. If desired, roll out additional dough and cut shapes with decorative cutters. Arrange cutouts on dough decoratively and brush them with egg wash. Chill fillet at least 1 hour and up to 2 hours, before baking.

Bake fillet in a preheated 400° oven for 30 minutes; reduce heat to 350°, and bake 5 to 10 minutes more, or until a meat thermometer registers 130° for medium-rare meat and the pastry is cooked through. Let stand for 15 minutes.

(continued)

Loosen fillet from pan, transfer it, using 2 spatulas, to a heated platter, and garnish it with watercress. Serve cut into ¾-inch-thick slices topped with Madeira Sauce. Makes 8 servings.

Madeira Sauce:

Reserved juice from fillet
½ cup Sercial Madeira
2 teaspoons arrowroot dissolved in
   1 teaspoon cold water
½ cup beef broth

2 tablespoons finely chopped black
   truffles (available at specialty food
   shops), if desired
Salt and pepper to taste

In a saucepan, boil reserved pan juices and Madeira until reduced by one quarter. Add arrowroot mixture, broth, and truffles. Season to taste with salt and pepper. Cook over moderate heat, stirring frequently, also being careful not to let it boil, for 5 minutes, or until thickened.

Chocolate Sauce:

⅓ cup each balsamic vinegar and maple
   syrup

1 tablespoon finely grated, unsweetened
   chocolate

Heat balsamic vinegar and maple syrup in small pan on medium-high. Once mixture simmers, reduce heat to medium-low. Simmer 5 to 8 minutes, until slightly thickened. Remove from heat. Stir in chocolate until melted, about 1 minute. Put fillet on a serving plate. Drizzle with sauce. Makes 2 servings.

Chateau Faire Le Pont Winery • www.fairelepont.com
Ohme Gardens

Gluten-Free London Broil

1 cup gluten-free Worcestershire sauce
1 cup gluten-free soy sauce
½ teaspoon ground ginger or 1 tablespoon grated fresh ginger
¼ cup sugar
⅛ cup seasoned salt
1 tablespoon chopped garlic
¼ cup water
½ cup white wine
2 bay leaves
Approximately 2 pounds flank steak

Combine all ingredients except flank steak; mix well. Pour over flank steak and marinate overnight. Grill steak to desired doneness and slice it thin.

J. J. Hills Fresh Grill
Icicle Village Resort

Mount Rainier

One of the most iconic images in America is of Mount Rainier. The highest point in Washington, Mount Rainier has three separate summits which 8,000 to 13,000 people attempt to reach every year. In addition to mountain climbers, Mount Rainier National Park welcomes over a million visitors annually.

Sadie Red Pot Roast

3 to 4 pound beef roast (chuck or sirloin roast works well)
Salt and pepper to taste
2 tablespoons canola oil
1 large onion, chopped
2 cloves garlic, chopped
1¼ cups red wine (Sadie Red is perfect for this recipe)
1 cup beef or vegetable broth
4 large carrots
2 to 3 large potatoes
1 (6-ounce) can tomato paste

Season meat with salt and pepper. Heat oil in a Dutch oven on medium-high heat; sear roast on all sides in oil until caramel brown in color, add onion and garlic and cook 5 minutes. Pour wine, broth and tomato paste over meat. (May add water if needed to cover.) Bring to simmer, cover with lid and roast in 400° oven 1 hour. After first hour reduce oven temperature to 300° and continue roasting 1½ hours. Add carrots and potatoes and return to oven 1 hour or until all ingredients are tender. Pair with Jacob Williams Cabernet or Merlot.

Julie Salcido
Jacob Williams Winery

Easy Beef Stroganoff

2 pounds boneless beef round, cut into 1-inch cubes
2 (10.75-ounce) cans cream of mushroom soup
1 medium onion, sliced
1 (8-ounce) container sour cream chive dip
3 cups hot cooked noodles

In large slow cooker, combine beef, soup and onion. Cover and cook on low 8 to 10 hours or on high 4 to 5 hours. Stir in dip. Serve over hot cooked noodles.

Swiss Steak

½ cup water
1 large round steak
2 (2-ounce) packets dry onion soup
    mix
¼ cup flour
5 (10.75-ounce) cans cream of
    mushroom soup
Pepper to taste

Preheat oven to 350°. Pour water in bottom of roasting pan. Slice round steak into large pieces, placing half into water. Sprinkle 1 package onion soup mix and flour on top of steaks. Pour 3 cans mushroom soup over flour. Place remaining steaks on top and sprinkle with remaining package onion soup mix. Top with remaining mushroom soup. Add pepper to taste. Bake, covered, 4 to 6 hours. Serve with mashed potatoes.

Jan Callahan
Dachshunds on Parade

Grandma Shirley's BBQ Brisket

1 brisket (NOT corned—usually vacuum packed)
1 (16-ounce) bottle Italian dressing (or 1 onion, sliced and 1 cup beef
   broth if making the same day)
Salt and pepper to taste

Trim excess fat off dense areas of meat. Put in roasting pan and punch holes in meat, pour Italian dressing over, chill overnight.

If cooking same day, put brisket in roasting pan, punch holes in meat, cover with sliced onion, add beef broth, salt and pepper.

Whether cooking overnight or same day, bake at 300° for 5 hours or until meat is tender. Serve with BBQ sauce or with gravy from drippings. Be sure to keep enough moisture in pan while baking.

Kent Cornucopia Days

Moon Dance Inn

Cascade Country Cook-Off

July

Stan Hedwall Park • Chehalis
www.cascadecookoff.com

The Cascade Country Cook-Off and Flea Market Fling is two huge days of smokin' barbecue, flea market finds, great music and incredible food. Held each July in beautiful Stan Hedwall Park, this barbecue and shopping utopia has something fun for everyone. On Saturday, chili cooks compete to create the perfect "Bowl of Red" and a chance to move on to the Tolbert Chili Championship in Terlingua, TX. Dutch Oven cooks pull out all the stops for a chance to compete at the World Dutch Oven Championship. On Sunday, the Pacific Northwest Barbecue Association sanctioned barbecue cook-off hosts teams from the U.S. and Canada for trophies, cash prizes and the opportunity to compete at the Jack Daniels World Championship Invitational Barbecue. Come for championship food and championship shopping. Tons of vendors come from all over, selling vintage, re-purposed and funky junque to delight the thrifty and crafty shopper.

Championship Low & Slow BBQ Beef Brisket

Day before cooking:

Beef brisket flat cut with ¼-inch fat cap on top side (ask butcher to leave it)
½ cup low-sodium soy sauce
¼ cup Worcestershire sauce
1 (1-ounce) packet au jus gravy mix
1 tablespoon hot sauce
2 (14-ounce) cans low-sodium beef broth

Score fat cap with sharp knife, in a grid pattern 1 inch apart. Combine remaining ingredients and mix well for marinade. Marinate or inject brisket with marinade. Cover and refrigerate to marinate overnight.

Day of cooking:

Yellow mustard
¼ cup brown sugar
1 tablespoon black pepper
1 tablespoon chili powder
1 tablespoon paprika
1 tablespoon garlic salt
1 teaspoon celery salt
¼ teaspoon allspice
¼ teaspoon thyme

Remove brisket from marinade and pat dry. Reserve marinade and set aside. Apply medium coat of yellow mustard to brisket. Don't worry, it will all disappear. Combine remaining ingredients, mixing well to create dry rub; coat liberally. In a baking pan or disposable aluminum pan, grill over indirect heat with light smoke from flavoring wood such as oak, hickory or mesquite. Stop smoke after 1 hour and keep cooking at 225° for 2 hours with fat cap up. Boil marinade 10 minutes. Flip brisket and baste with cooked marinade to keep beef moist. Continue cooking, flipping and basting every hour for approximately 1¾ hours per pound or to an internal temperature of 190°. Slice ¼-inch thick, against the grain. Use remaining cooked marinade and pan drippings to dredge brisket slices before serving.

Patt Maddock, Maddog's BBQ.
Cascade Country Cook-Off

Applesauce Meatloaf

¾ cup applesauce, seasoned and ready to eat
1½ pounds ground beef
¾ cup fine dry breadcrumbs
6 tablespoons ketchup
¾ teaspoon salt
¼ teaspoon sage

Combine all ingredients and mix well. Shape into loaf and bake at 350°
for 50 minutes.

Helen Louise Fort England, deceased, 2nd generation volunteer
Manson Apple Blossom Festival

Manson Apple Blossom Festival

Swedish Meatballs
(Köttbullar)

1 cup breadcrumbs
1 cup milk
1½ pounds ground beef
1 pound ground pork
1 medium onion, chopped fine
2 eggs, beaten
2 tablespoons Worcestershire sauce
½ cup grated Parmesan cheese
Salt, pepper, fresh garlic or garlic powder to taste
Butter for frying

In a large bowl, soak breadcrumbs in milk until most of the milk is incorporated. Add beef, pork, onion, eggs, Worcestershire, cheese and spices to soaked breadcrumbs, working all ingredients together. Let mixture rest 1 hour in refrigerator. Form into small balls about 1 to 1½ inches in diameter. Brown meatballs in butter in frying pan. Add enough water to cover bottom quarter of meatballs and cook 30 minutes. Meatballs are served with boiled potatoes, gravy and lingonberry preserves.

Margaret Lidberg
Nordic Heritage Museum

Spicy Joes

1½ pounds ground beef
1 large onion, chopped
1 garlic clove, minced
1 (6-ounce) can spicy vegetable juice
½ cup ketchup
½ cup water

2 tablespoons brown sugar
2 tablespoons chopped canned
   jalapeño peppers
1 tablespoon prepared mustard
2 teaspoons chili powder
1 teaspoon Worcestershire sauce

In a large skillet brown ground beef, onion and garlic; drain. In large pot combine vegetable juice, ketchup, water, brown sugar, jalapeño peppers, mustard, chili powder and Worcestershire sauce. Stir in meat mixture. Heat over medium-high heat for 10 minutes, reduce heat and simmer 25 minutes. Serve warm on buns with favorite cheese.

Lettuce Wraps

1 pound ground pork or turkey	⅓ cup lime juice
½ cup chopped onion	½ cup soy sauce
2 teaspoons ginger (fresh or from a jar)	¼ cup cilantro
	½ cup chopped peanuts
2 teaspoons minced garlic (fresh or from a jar)	Lettuce
	Shredded cheese (optional)

Brown meat with onion; drain if needed. Remove from heat and add ginger, garlic, lime juice, soy sauce, cilantro and peanuts, mixing well. Spoon mixture evenly onto lettuce leaves, sprinkle with cheese and roll up.

Note: Good types of lettuce to use are iceberg, red lettuce, radicchio or large spinach leaves. Dry lettuce well before using in the wraps.

Bridgid Kardong, wife of Bloomsday Race Director Don Kardong
Lilac Bloomsday Run

North Shore Lasagna

1 pound ground beef
½ cup chopped yellow onion
1 (24-ounce) package lasagna noodles
1 (29-ounce) can tomato sauce
1 (16-ounce) carton cottage cheese
1 (29-ounce) can diced tomatoes with green chilies
1 (4-ounce) can sliced black olives
1 teaspoon salt
1 teaspoon pepper
1 teaspoon chili powder
2 cups shredded mozzarella cheese
2 cups shredded Cheddar cheese

Brown ground beef with onion; drain. Break pasta in half and add to boiling water. Cook 10 minutes and drain. In large bowl combine tomato sauce, cottage cheese, diced tomatoes, olives, salt, pepper, chili powder and ground beef mixture. Layer pasta, sauce, mozzarella and Cheddar until pan is full, ending with cheeses. Bake at 350° for 30 minutes or until cheese is thoroughly melted.

Ginny Hill, North Shore Grill
Razor Clam Festival

Creekside Lasagne

1 pound ground beef
½ cup chopped onion
1 (8-ounce) can tomato sauce
1 (6-ounce) can tomato paste
1 cup water
1 (4-ounce) can sliced mushrooms
2 cloves mashed garlic
¾ teaspoon oregano

¾ teaspoon basil
1 (14-ounce) can spinach
1 egg beaten
¾ cup cottage cheese
¼ cup grated Parmesan cheese
1⅓ cups shredded mozzarella
   cheese, divided
10 lasagna noodles

Brown ground beef with onion, add tomato sauce and paste, water, mushrooms and seasonings. Combine spinach, egg, cottage cheese, Parmesan and 1 cup mozzarella. Pour some meat sauce in baking dish, layer with noodles and cottage cheese mixture. Repeat layers, finishing last layer with remaining mozzarella. Bake uncovered for 25 minutes at 350°.

Wine pairing suggestion: Scatter Creek's Creekside Rossa Pinot Noir.

Scatter Creek Winery

Washington Easy Hot Dish

1 pound ground beef
2 (10.75-ounce) cans cream of potato soup
1 (10.75-ounce) can cream of celery soup
1½ cans milk, using soup cans to measure
Salt and pepper to taste
1 (30-ounce) package frozen hash brown potatoes

Brown meat and drain. Add soups, milk, salt and pepper; mix well. Place in large casserole dish. Spread hash browns on top. Bake at 350° for 45 minutes or until crisp on top.

String Pie

2 teaspoons butter
1 pound ground beef
½ cup chopped onion
½ cup chopped green pepper
1 (15-ounce) jar spaghetti sauce
8 ounces spaghetti
2 eggs, beaten
1 cup cottage cheese
⅓ cup grated Parmesan cheese
¾ cup shredded mozzarella cheese

Preheat oven to 350°. Grease 9x13-inch casserole dish with butter and set aside. Brown ground beef in skillet, add onion and green pepper. Cook until done, drain fat; add spaghetti sauce and simmer 15 minutes. Cook spaghetti until almost done; drain. Add spaghetti to skillet and mix well; cool slightly. Mix beaten eggs with cottage cheese and Parmesan cheese. Carefully fold into beef mixture. Pour into casserole dish, top with mozzarella cheese and bake 20 minutes until cheese is browned and gooey. Serves 6.

Sedro-Woolley Loggerodeo

Lamb Braised in Zinfandel

2 to 3 tablespoons olive oil
2½ pounds lamb shoulder or leg, cubed
3 to 4 tablespoons flour
1¼ cup Maryhill Reserve Zinfandel,
   divided
1 cup beef stock
8 to 10 ounces tomato sauce

Rosemary to taste
Salt and pepper to taste
1 cup diced celery
1 cup chopped onion
4 to 6 ounces canned mushroom pieces
½ cup fresh chopped parsley

In a Dutch oven or other heavy kettle, heat oil, brown lamb, sprinkle flour over meat and stir well. Add half the wine and all the beef stock and tomato sauce; cook, stirring constantly, until it boils and thickens (add more wine if needed). Add rosemary, salt, pepper, celery and onion; cover and simmer gently 1 hour. Shortly before serving stir in mushrooms, parsley and remaining Zinfandel, simmer a short while. Serve over rough-smashed Yukon Gold potatoes.

Maryhill Winery

Elk Medallions with Huckleberry Sauce

½ cup garlic
½ cup shallots, chopped
2 pounds huckleberries
2 cups cranberry juice
1 cup apple cider vinegar
2 pounds honey
4 tablespoons fresh thyme

2 tablespoons rubbed sage
2 teaspoons kosher salt
1 teaspoon white pepper
4½ cups water, divided
½ cup cornstarch
3 (4-ounce) elk medallion tenderloins

Add garlic and shallots to sauté pan with a drizzle of oil; brown. In a large pot, combine garlic mixture, huckleberries, cranberry juice, cider vinegar, honey, thyme, sage, salt, pepper and 4 cups water; bring to a boil. Reduce heat and simmer for approximately 15 minutes. Combine cornstarch with ½ cup water; stir into sauce to thicken. Put sauce aside. Sear or grill tenderloins to desired temperature (medium-rare is recommended for best tenderness). Serve elk on top of potatoes or rice, top with huckleberry sauce and serve with vegetables.

Summit House Restaurant, Crystal Mountain Resort

Summit House Restaurant

Courtesy of Crystal Mountain Resort

360-663-3085
www.CrystalMountainResort.com

The Summit House is Washington's highest elevation restaurant perched at 6,872 feet above sea level at Crystal Mountain Resort. The menu features a wide selection of fresh Northwest cuisine, wine, spirits, beer and other refreshments in an elegant alpine setting. Guests can enjoy fresh local seafood, steaks, burgers, roasted chicken and gourmet salads. During the summer there's also a casual outdoor patio where guests can breathe in the fresh mountain air as they dine. There are breathtaking 360-degree views of the Cascade Range, including a view of Mt. Rainier. The dining experience begins with the Mt. Rainier Gondola, traveling almost 2,500 vertical feet to the top, soaring over Evergreen trees, wildlife and lush meadows of wildflowers during the summer, and skiers buzzing by below during the winter. It is truly an unforgettable dining experience.

The Culinary Madman's Venison Medallions with Blackberry Sauce

1 tablespoon olive oil
1 pound venison tenderloin, sliced into medallions
1 tablespoon balsamic vinegar
5 ounces beef stock
2 tablespoons red currant jelly
1 clove garlic, minced or grated with a ribbon grater
½ cup blackberries
Salt and pepper to taste

Heat oil in skillet on medium-high heat, season venison medallions and cook to desired doneness. Remove venison from pan and set aside to rest. Add balsamic vinegar to pan to deglaze, then add beef stock, red currant jelly and garlic. Whisk sauce together and add blackberries and cook until berries are soft. Salt and pepper to taste. Plate venison, pour sauce over and enjoy!

Jess Owen, The Culinary Madman
Certified Culinary Consultant
Assistant General Manager
Ocean Crest Resort
1-800-684-8439

Chocolate Pulled Pork Sliders with Chocolate BBQ Sauce

Favorite dry rub   1 pork shoulder
2 tablespoons cocoa powder

Preheat oven to 425°. In a small bowl, combine dry rub and cocoa powder. Dust both sides of pork shoulder with dry rub. Place pork on rack in roasting pan. Roast 20 minutes, reduce heat to 325°. Cook 4 hours or until thermometer inserted into shoulder reads 185°. Remove from oven and let stand 30 minutes. Reserve drippings for sauce. Shred pork.

Chocolate BBQ Sauce:

1 tablespoon pork fat   ¼ cup cider vinegar
½ onion, chopped fine   ¼ cup packed brown sugar
2 garlic cloves, minced   4½ teaspoons Worcestershire sauce
¼ teaspoon chili powder   ¼ teaspoon pepper
⅔ cup ketchup   ¼ cup pork drippings
6 tablespoons brewed coffee   ½ cup chocolate syrup

Combine pork fat and onion in saucepan. Cook over medium heat until onion softens, about 10 minutes. Add garlic and chili powder. Cook 30 seconds. Stir in remaining ingredients except chocolate syrup and simmer until thickened, about 15 minutes. Remove from heat. Stir in chocolate syrup.

Chocolate BBQ Sauce is typically better if allowed to sit overnight in the refrigerator. Warm sauce gently and add to warmed pulled pork. If you just can't wait, go ahead and add it to pulled pork and serve on slider rolls.

Jess Owen, Ocean Crest Resort Owner/Former Executive Chef
2009 2nd Place Winner, Savory Professionals CotBF Recipe Contest
Chocolate on the Beach Festival

Apricot Pulled Pork

3 to 3½ pound boneless pork shoulder roast
1 (10-ounce) jar apricot spreadable fruit
1 cup bottled hot-style barbecue sauce
½ cup chopped sweet onion
½ cup snipped dried apricots

Lightly coat large slow cooker with nonstick cooking spray. Trim fat from meat and place in cooker (may cut however necessary to fit). In medium bowl combine spreadable fruit, barbecue sauce, onion and dried apricots. Pour over meat. Cook on low 8 to 10 hours or on high 4 to 5 hours. Gently shred meat and serve as main dish with vegetables or as a sandwich.

Apple Cup Café

Carnitas Michoacan Style

SOUTH is located in Leavenworth at 913 Front Street and in Wenatchee in the Pybus Public Market. Carnitas Michoacan Style is one of their most popular dishes.

Enough lard to submerge pork
5 pounds pork shoulder or leg, cut
   into fist-size pieces
Juice of 1½ oranges

Juice of 1 lime
1 cup cola
½ teaspoon ground cumin
2 tablespoons salt

In a large pot heat ½ cup lard until melted and sizzling but not smoking. Add pork to pot, 1 piece at a time, being sure not to crowd or stack meat. Turn from side to side as each side browns. Continue working in batches until all meat is browned. Return all meat to pot; add additional lard and heat on medium until lard melts and covers pork. Combine remaining ingredients and mix well. When lard begins to boil add orange mixture. Continue cooking over medium heat, stirring occasionally so meat does not stick. Simmer until meat becomes tender enough to pull apart. Remove meat from lard and drain on paper towels. Pull chunks apart into bite-size pieces and serve with salsa and warm tortillas.

Martin Romero, South Restaurant • www.southrestaurants.com
Cascade Farmlands

Visit Leavenworth

North Central Washington is home to outstanding ag-tourism and culinary destinations. Wineries, artisan food makers, world famous tree fruit orchards and organic farms dot the region. Among these remarkable attractions, visitors stop in Leavenworth, Washington's Bavarian Village. Made over to reflect a Bavarian theme in the 1960's, Leavenworth has become an international tourist destination. The village offers all things authentic, including the German cuisine. Visit Leavenworth to sample sausages and kraut, wienerschnitzel and a complete menu of Bavarian favorites.

Culinary review of Leavenworth
submitted by Cascade Farmlands

Rib, Chicken and Sausage Bake

3 pounds pork spare ribs
3 pounds chicken pieces
3 pounds sausage (half hot and half
   sweet), skin pricked
3 medium onions, sliced
¾ cup ketchup
¾ cup water
1 tablespoon salt
1 tablespoon sugar

2 tablespoons vinegar
2 tablespoons Worcestershire sauce
2 tablespoons lemon juice
1 teaspoon chili powder
1 teaspoon paprika
½ teaspoon hot pepper sauce
½ teaspoon pepper
Pinch of oregano
Pinch of sweet basil

Preheat oven to 300°. Cut ribs into 2-rib portions. Place in large Dutch oven; add enough water to cover. Heat to boiling, cover and cook 15 minutes. Remove ribs. Put chicken pieces in large roasting pan, add spare ribs and sausages. Top with sliced onions. In small bowl combine remaining ingredients and pour over meat in roasting pan. Cover and bake 1½ hours. Remove from oven and spoon off fat.

Artie Werner
Foss Waterway Seaport

Slow Cooker Cranberry Ribs

2 teaspoons ground cumin
2 teaspoons chili powder
2 teaspoons packed brown sugar
3 to 3½ pounds pork loin back ribs
1 (16-ounce) can whole-berry cranberry sauce, divided
1 (12-ounce) jar beef gravy
2 tablespoons cider vinegar
2 tablespoons packed brown sugar
1 teaspoon salt
½ teaspoon crushed red pepper flakes
2 cloves garlic, chopped

Line broiler pan with foil. In small bowl, combine cumin, chili powder and brown sugar. Rub evenly over ribs. Place on rack in broiler pan. Broil with tops 4 to 6 inches from heat for 10 to 15 minutes, turning once until browned. Cool slightly. Cut into individual ribs. Place ribs in large slow cooker. In medium bowl, mix half the cranberry sauce and remaining ingredients together; pour over ribs.

Cook on high 3 hours or until tender. Stir in remaining half of cranberry sauce; stir well. Ribs will hold on low for up to 2 hours.

Oven-Braised Short Ribs in Wine

4 to 5 pounds bone-in beef short ribs	2 cloves garlic, split
Salt and pepper to taste	1 (14.5-ounce) can diced tomatoes, drained
2 tablespoons olive oil	1 cup Wind Rose Dolcetto wine
½ red or yellow onion, diced	1 teaspoon black pepper
2 carrots, peeled and diced	½ (14.5-ounce) can stock beef stock
2 stalks celery with leaves, diced	1 bunch flat-leaf Italian parsley, divided

Preheat oven to 325°. Season short ribs with salt and pepper. Heat oil in large Dutch oven over medium-high. Divide ribs into 2 or 3 batches so ribs are not overcrowded. Sear to a nice color on all sides. Transfer ribs to another plate or bowl. Reduce heat to medium; add onion, carrots and celery to pot, stirring often until vegetables begin to glisten and onions begin to appear transparent. Add garlic and continue cooking 3 to 4 more minutes. Add drained tomatoes; continue cooking until tomatoes begin to break down and become incorporated with other vegetables, about 8 to 10 minutes. Add 1 cup Dolcetto, raise heat and boil or simmer until wine begins to reduce. Add black pepper, stock and half the chopped parsley. Bring to boil again, add ribs, cover and place in preheated oven. Cook until ribs are fork tender, about 2½ hours. Transfer ribs to platter. Strain liquid, remove fat from surface and continue cooking on stove top to reduce stock until sauce forms, check seasoning and add ribs back to coat with sauce prior to serving. Garnish with remaining chopped parsley.

Wind Rose Cellars

Wind Rose Cellars

The tasting room is open year round.

143 West Washington • Sequim
360-681-0690 • www.windrosecellars.com

Wind Rose Cellars, located on the Olympic Peninsula in sunny Sequim, has a passion for producing premium wines made from grapes grown in Washington State. They produce big Italian reds including Dolcetto, Barbera, Primitivo, Nebbiolo, and delicious whites such as Pinot Grigio and Moscato. Many of the wines are produced in small lots, often numbering fewer than two hundred cases per wine. Each wine can stand alone, but the acidity balance is crafted to complement food.

The 2011 Dolcetto used in the recipe is crafted in the traditional style, never touching any oak. The wine is a deep purple with aromas of raspberry jam, shaved chocolate and fresh mulberries. Natural tannins support this medium body dry wine.

Corn Daugs

Mom got this recipe from a carnival vendor over 60 years ago. Absolutely the best!

1 cup yellow cornmeal	1 egg
1 cup sifted flour	1¼ cups milk
2 tablespoons baking powder	Wooden skewers
1 teaspoon salt	1 (8-count) package hot dogs

Combine cornmeal, flour, baking powder and salt. Add egg and milk; mix until smooth, about 1 minute.

Skewer hot dogs, roll in mixture and deep fry at 375° until golden.

Kathy McKean
Dachshunds on Parade

Dachshunds on Parade

3rd Saturday in June

iStockphoto/thinkstock

Main Street • Ellensburg
509-925-3137 • 888-925-2204
www.dachshundsonparade.com

Dachshunds on Parade in Ellensburg has grown from a Central Washington University class project into one of Ellensburg's most popular events. Each year over 200 dogs and their owners show up to celebrate the love of dachshunds. The day begins with a breakfast with the dogs and continues with a costume contest, a short parade, and pet tricks, followed by the always entertaining dachshund races. The dachshund races feature 4 dogs racing at once and no one can predict what will happen once the race starts! Some dogs run, some don't, and some run half way and turn around. The only guarantee is that you will be entertained. Dachshunds on Parade is a free event and all are welcome.

Chorizo and Lentil Étouffée

2 tablespoons vegetable oil
¾ cup diced carrots
1½ cups diced bell pepper
2 tablespoons sliced serrano peppers
1 tablespoon garlic, chopped
2 (14.5-ounce) cans tomato, diced
2 cups chicken stock
3 tablespoons smoked paprika
2½ tablespoons cocoa powder

3 tablespoons ground coffee
1 pound pre-cooked chorizo sausage
  links
2¼ cups water, divided
½ cup black beluga lentils
½ cup jasmine rice
1 teaspoon cumin, ground
Salt and pepper to taste
Scallions, thinly sliced

Heat oil in large pot or Dutch oven over medium-high heat until it begins to smoke slightly; add carrots, peppers and garlic. Cook until softened. Add tomatoes and chicken stock to vegetables and bring to a simmer. Blend smoked paprika, cocoa powder and ground coffee together and add to pot. If cocoa powder and smoked paprika are clumpy, sift over pot when adding. Slice chorizo sausage into rounds and add to pot. Simmer 45 minutes.

In medium saucepan, bring 1¼ cups water to a boil and add lentils; cover and reduce to simmer. Cook 15 to 20 minutes, until tender. Drain lentils and set aside. In a medium saucepan, bring 1 cup water to a boil and add rice, cover and reduce heat to low for 18 minutes. In a medium bowl, mix lentils and rice with cumin; add salt and pepper.

To serve, top lentil-rice mixture with sausage mixture. Garnish with scallions.

Allen Skelton
National Lentil Festival

Salmon, Shrimp and Scallop Bake

1 stick butter, melted
½ cup mayonnaise
½ small red onion, cut in small chunks
1 medium red bell pepper, chopped in
   small pieces
1 (2.25-ounce) can sliced black olives,
   drained
3 teaspoons capers

½ teaspoon garlic
½ teaspoon dried red pepper flakes
4 (5-ounce) salmon fillets
1 teaspoon fresh dill
8 large shrimp, peeled
4 large scallops
1 small lemon cut into four slices

Combine melted butter and mayonnaise, mixing well. Add onion, red bell pepper, olives, capers, garlic and red pepper flakes; mix until well incorporated. Place each salmon fillet on large piece of aluminum foil. Sprinkle with fresh dill. Spoon mayonnaise mixture on top. Place 2 peeled shrimp on top of each salmon and 1 large scallop on top of shrimp. Spoon more mayonnaise mixture on top. Add a slice of lemon. Fold aluminum foil around salmon, sealing sides and top. Bake at 450° for 30 minutes. Serve with garlic French bread, salad and Glacier Peak Siegerrebe.

Chef Hank of Norwesting Magazine
Glacier Peak Winery

Brand X Pictures/thinkstock

Glacier Peak Winery

58575 St Route 20 at Hwy Marker 104 • Rockport
360-873-4073 • www.glacierpeakwinery.com

Glacier Peak Winery is located in the Upper Skagit Valley in the town of Rockport. Surrounded by the Majestic Mountain Peaks of the Cascades and Skagit River, where the Great Bald Eagle comes to nest each winter. The vineyard grows a variety of grapes such as Pinot Noir, Agria, Siegerrebe, and the Madeleine Angevine. In addition, Glacier Peak Winery bottles Merlot, Cabernet Sauvignon, Syrah and sweet dessert wines produced from grapes grown in premium Washington vineyards. Come visit the tasting room and enjoy the relaxing surroundings.

If traveling during July, definitely come celebrate the 4th with a barbeque and concert at the winery. A choice of steak or salmon is served, the festivities kick off at 5pm.

Linda's Succulent Sautéed Shrimp

1 pound raw shrimp
¼ cup butter
2 teaspoons lemon juice
1 teaspoon parsley flakes
1 teaspoon chives

¾ teaspoon seasoned salt
½ teaspoon garlic powder
½ teaspoon dry mustard
½ teaspoon tarragon leave
⅛ teaspoon red pepper

Shell and devein shrimp. Add to melted butter in skillet. Add lemon juice and seasonings. Sauté over medium heat 8 minutes or until pink. Serve hot over rice.

Kent Cornucopia Days

Grilled Salmon with Lavender and Basil

4 fresh salmon fillets
5 large basil leaves, chopped
2 tablespoons tamari soy sauce
2 tablespoons lemon juice
⅓ cup olive oil
Salt and pepper to taste

Wash salmon, pat dry and set aside. Combine remaining ingredients, pour over salmon, cover and let rest in refrigerator 1 hour. Place salmon on hot, lightly oiled grill or barbeque, skin side down. When salmon is done, remove from grill and serve.

Pelindaba Lavender®

Salmon Baked On a Spit

Clean fish (local coastal salmon is the best), season inside with salt and pepper. Insert a 30-inch spit along the backbone of a 6- to 8-pound salmon. Balance fish so it will turn easily. Adjust forks and tighten screws. Using a piece of chicken wire, fold this around fish with metal skewers (a sturdy aluminum foil will also work bunched up around fish). This prevents flesh from falling off the bones while cooking. Have spit about 8 inches from slow coals and/or cedar wood chips. Start turning and cook 1 to 1½ hours or until fish flakes easily when tested with a fork. Serve with lemon and/or your favorite sauce.

Museum of the North Beach

Salmon Casserole
(Finland)

3 large potatoes, peeled and sliced
1 pound cooked salmon (tail end, thinly sliced)
1 small onion, sliced
Salt, black pepper, fresh cut dill to taste
2 eggs
2 cups half-and-half
Butter

Butter a 1½-quart casserole dish. Place half of potatoes on bottom. Cover with fish and onion. Sprinkle salt, pepper and dill over fish. Cover with remaining potatoes. Combine eggs with half-and-half; beat well. Pour egg mixture over potatoes and fish layers. Dot with butter. Bake at 350° for 1 hour or until slightly browned.

Benita Westerberg
Nordic Heritage Museum

Whole Salmon with Lime, Cilantro and Jalapeño

1 whole salmon (7 to 9 pounds with head removed)
Kosher salt to taste
Fresh cracked pepper to taste
1 bunch cilantro, chopped

2 limes, thinly sliced and seeded
10 slices jalapeño
2 cloves garlic, minced
6 tablespoons olive oil

Set up grill for indirect grilling and preheat to medium. If using charcoal grill, place drip pan in center. If using gas grill, place wood chips, if desired, in smoker box or in a smoker pouch and preheat to high until smoke appears. Reduce heat to medium. Cut large piece of cardboard into rectangle as long and wide as fish. Wrap cardboard in several layers of aluminum foil; set aside. Remove gills and fins from fish, trim tail. Rinse fish, inside and out, under cold running water; drain and blot dry, inside and out, with paper towels. Make 4 or 5 diagonal slashes to bone in each side of fish. Season cavity with salt and pepper. Stuff cavity and slashes with half the cilantro and lime, tucking jalapeños into sides. Stir remaining cilantro and garlic into olive oil with any remaining jalapeños and salt to taste. Brush fish on both sides with oil mixture. Place fish on aluminum-wrapped cardboard. Place in center of hot coals, away from heat, and cover. Baste every 15 minutes with oil mixture until fish is done, approximately 45 minutes.

Polly Barber
South Sound BBQ Festival

South Sound BBQ Festival

July • Saturday following Independence Day

Huntamer Park • Lacey
360-491-4141
www.southsoundbbqfestival.com

The South Sound BBQ Festival, hosted by the Lacey Chamber of Commerce, is the premier event for BBQ lovers in South Puget Sound. This event features professional chefs from around the state showing off their BBQ expertise and allows the nearly 10,000 guests an opportunity to purchase tastes for as little as $2.00. Headlining the festival is a competition of amateur BBQ aficionados submitting samples of their culinary masterpieces in up to 5 categories. Several northwest Native American tribes compete in a salmon cook-off using traditional tribal cooking methods and host a non-competitive display of tribal culture. Contestants in the chicken wing eating contest are judged on the weight of wings eaten in 4 minutes. Complete with music, children's activities and free admission, the South Sound BBQ Festival definitely has something for everyone.

Marv's E-Z Money Salmon

"A guaranteed return on your investment"

2 tablespoons unsalted butter
1 tablespoon soy sauce
2 crushed garlic cloves
1 teaspoon hot pepper flakes
Black pepper to taste
1 teaspoon chopped fresh rosemary
1 teaspoon chopped fresh oregano
1 fresh salmon fillet

Fire up the grill. Combine butter, soy sauce, garlic, peppers and herbs in microwavable bowl. Heat on high until butter melts, about 1 minute. Debone salmon and place on platter skin side down. Spoon butter mixture over salmon and refrigerate until butter hardens. Grill, skin side down, until salmon is cooked through.

South Sound BBQ Festival

Seared Scallops with Viognier Reduction Sauce

High temperature oil for searing
8 big scallops, completely thawed and
    patted dry
Salt and pepper to taste
½ cup Cougar Crest Viognier wine

2 tablespoons diced shallots
1 teaspoon butter
½ cup diced peach
1 teaspoon Dijon mustard
1 teaspoon orange zest

Place thin layer of oil in large pan and bring to medium-high heat. Make sure oil is completely hot, pat scallops dry again, season with salt and pepper on both sides and place in pan. Sear at least 1 minute until golden brown and crispy. Turn and sear other side. Remove scallops from pan and reduce heat to low. Add wine, shallots, butter and peach, scraping pan to release brown bits. Heat until liquid is reduced by a third. Add Dijon mustard and orange zest, stir to heat through, and pour over scallops. Serve as a main dish with rice or other starch, or on top of a salad, or as an appetizer.

Deborah Hansen
Cougar Crest Estate Winery

Cougar Crest Estate Winery

50 Frenchtown Road • Walla Walla
509-529-5980 • www.cougarcrestwinery.com

Cougar Crest Estate Winery is a family owned boutique winery in the southeast corner of Washington, in the Walla Walla Valley. Owners Dave and Debbie Hansen raise 60 acres of wine grapes on the estate. Their winery is a beautiful Prairie-style building with expansive views of the countryside, seven miles west of the town of Walla Walla. The interior is spacious, with  soaring ceilings, clerestory windows, chunky gluelam beams, and barrel rolled ceilings lined with wood. Seating is modern and comfortable and the tasting bar is large enough to accommodate any size group. In addition to daily wine tasting, there are bocce ball and horseshoe courts. Expansive patios with plenty of seating make a picnic at the winery possible any day of the week. Visitors will find a truly personalized visit with attentive staff and the opportunity to experience small town hospitality as only Cougar Crest can offer.

Fried Razor Clams

15 cleaned razor clams
Salt and pepper to taste
1 cup flour
1 cup panko (Japanese breadcrumbs)

1 tablespoon basil flakes
3 eggs, beaten
Oil for frying

Rinse clams, drain and pat dry. In medium bowl, combine salt, pepper and flour; mix well and set aside. In a separate bowl, combine panko and basil flakes and set aside. Dip clam pieces into flour, then into eggs, and roll in panko mixture. Pour oil ¼-inch deep in pan and heat to medium-high. Place clams in oil and brown 1 minute. Flip and brown an additional minute. Razor clams cook quickly and will be tough if cooked too long. Remove and drain on paper towels. Serve immediately.

Museum of the North Beach

Clam Fritters

1 pound razor clams, minced
½ cup diced onion
1 egg
¾ cup pancake mix
¼ teaspoon fresh ground black pepper
½ teaspoon kosher salt

Mix all ingredients together, cover and refrigerate for 30 minutes. In large frying pan place ½ cup batter and spread to size of an English muffin, about 3½ inches in diameter. Cook on each side till golden brown.

Razor Clam Festival

Baked Clams

12 clams
3 tablespoons butter, divided
¼ cup finely chopped onion
1 clove garlic, peeled and
    crushed

1 egg, slightly beaten
¼ cup plus ⅓ cup dry, seasoned
    breadcrumbs, divided
⅛ teaspoon dried oregano leaves

Remove clams from half shell and chop coarsely. Set clams and shells aside. In a microwaveable mixing bowl place 2 tablespoons butter. Heat on low in microwave 30 seconds or until melted. Add onion and garlic. Heat, uncovered, in microwave 3 minutes or until onion is tender. Add egg, ¼ cup breadcrumbs, chopped clams and oregano to mixture. Spoon mixture into reserved shells. Place shells on baking pan. In a small bowl combine ⅓ cup breadcrumbs and 2 tablespoons butter, melted. Sprinkle buttered breadcrumbs on top of clam mixture. Bake clams at 350° for 25 minutes or until golden brown.

Pacific Razor Clam Ceviche with Black Chocolate Oil and Blood Orange Supremes

Ceviche:

1 pound Pacific razor clams
2 red jalapeños
4 tablespoons cilantro
¼ small red onion, thinly sliced
2 tablespoons extra virgin olive oil
1½ cups fresh-squeezed lemon juice

1½ cups fresh-squeezed lime juice
1 cup fresh-squeezed blood orange juice
1 blood orange, for supremes (slices)
Coarse sea salt

Wash clams well. Thinly slice clams horizontally; set aside. Remove seeds from jalapeños and chop fine. Wash hands after this step to remove any remaining jalapeño juice. Remove cilantro leaves from stems and roughly chop leaves. Combine jalapeños, cilantro, onion and olive oil in large glass, ceramic or stainless steel bowl. Add lemon, lime and blood orange juices. Mix well and add sliced clams. Cover and refrigerate for at least 1 hour, but no more than 24 hours.

Black Chocolate Oil:

¼ cup dark, unsweetened Dutch cocoa powder

½ cup extra virgin olive oil
2 tablespoons real maple syrup

Combine all ingredients in small bowl. Whisk until smooth.

Once ceviche is thoroughly chilled, softened and broken up a bit from soaking, place on plate with blood orange slices, drizzle with chocolate oil and coarse sea salt. Serve alone or with tortilla chips.

Andrew Bickar, Ocean Crest Resort Executive Chef
Chocolate on the Beach Festival

Fresh Oyster Casserole

2 tablespoons melted butter
1 (3-ounce) can French fried onions,
  divided
1½ pint shucked, drained oysters

¼ cup light cream
2 tablespoons grated Parmesan
  cheese
2 tablespoons butter

Add melted butter to a deep casserole dish. Cover bottom with half the can of French fried onions. Add oysters and light cream. In a bowl, combine Parmesan cheese and remaining half can French fried onions; spread on top of oysters. Dot with butter. Bake at 450° for 8 to 10 minutes or until oyster edges begin to curl.

Skipper Kincaid
Oysterfest

Oysterfest

1st weekend in October

Shelton • www.oysterfest.org

Oysters, wines, microbrews, live music and so much more come together for two days every year for Oysterfest. Hosted by the Shelton Skookum Rotary Club Foundation and attended by thousands, OysterFest is home to the West Coast Oyster Shucking Championships and is Washington State's official seafood festival. The festival also features a popular cook-off, hands-on water quality exhibits, and a giant food pavilion with nearly 100 unique items on the menu: BBQ oysters, fritters, spring rolls, garlic shrimp, fresh cider and so much more. Better yet, this culinary adventure supports about 100 local non-profit service clubs and organizations, as well as funding scholarships and local community improvement projects. What hidden pearls will you find at OysterFest?

Dungeness Crab Enchiladas

2 tablespoons olive oil
1 medium yellow onion, chopped
2 shallots, chopped
1 jalapeño pepper, seeded and chopped
1 clove garlic, finely chopped
1 teaspoon cumin
Juice of 1 lime
8 ounces grated Monterey Jack cheese, divided
¾ pound Dungeness crabmeat
1 (8-ounce) can enchilada sauce
1 dozen corn tortillas
½ cup vegetable oil
8 ounces grated Tillamook cheese
½ cup scallions, sliced in thin rounds
1 (2-ounce) can sliced olives
¼ cup fresh cilantro, chopped

Preheat oven to 325°. Heat olive oil in skillet over medium heat. Add chopped onion, shallots and jalapeño; cook until onion is translucent. Add garlic, cumin and lime juice. Let cool and stir in half the Monterey Jack cheese and all the crab. Heat enchilada sauce in separate skillet and dip corn tortillas in sauce only long enough to soften. Using a cutting board, fill each tortilla with crab mixture and roll up. Place filled tortillas in 9x13-inch nonstick baking pan tightly, side by side. Evenly pour enchilada sauce over tortillas. Sprinkle with remaining Monterey Jack cheese and Tillamook cheese. Bake 20 minutes. Garnish with scallions, olives and cilantro.

Museum of the North Beach

Dungeness Crab Quiche

4 large eggs
2 cups heavy cream
2 tablespoons finely chopped fresh chives
2 tablespoons finely chopped fresh parsley
½ teaspoon salt
¼ teaspoon black pepper
⅛ teaspoon freshly grated nutmeg
½ cup coarsely grated Monterey Jack cheese
½ cup coarsely grated Swiss cheese
1 pound fresh Dungeness crabmeat
1 prebaked pie crust

Preheat oven to 375°. Whisk together eggs, cream, herbs, salt, pepper and nutmeg. Stir in cheeses and crabmeat. Pour into prebaked crust and bake 40 minutes or until filling puffs and is no longer wobbly in center when gently shaken, 40 to 50 minutes. Cool in pie plate on rack 15 minutes before serving.

Kim Roberts, Westport Winery
Westport Art Festival

Westport Art Festival

3rd weekend in August
Saturday: 10am to 6pm • Sunday: 10am to 4pm

Westport Maritime Museum • Westport
800-345-6223
www.westportartfestival.org

There's nothing better than good old-fashioned fun with a class act experience! That is what visitors experience at the Westport Art Festival. Eighty vendors, representing the best in art, entertainment and food will be waiting at the Marina District in Westport. Activities appeal to all types of interests, from paintings, jewelry, pottery and belly dancing, there is something for everyone. A backdrop of the beautiful Westport Marina, set against the Olympic Mountains and historic Port of Grays Harbor, is the perfect setting for strolling, shopping, tasting and fun. For more information contact the Westport/Grayland Chamber of Commerce.

Dungeness Crab Salad Sandwiches

¾ pound Dungeness crabmeat
1 cup shredded Cheddar cheese
½ cup finely chopped celery
2 tablespoons shallots or scallions, finely minced
⅔ cup chopped parsley
½ cup mayonnaise
1 tablespoon lemon juice
1 teaspoon Dijon mustard
⅛ teaspoon Tabasco
4 English muffins

Combine crabmeat, cheese, celery, shallots and parsley; mix well and set aside. Combine mayonnaise, lemon juice, mustard and Tabasco. Toss crabmeat mixture with mayonnaise mixture. Halve each English muffin, spread mixture on muffins. Broil about 4 inches from heat for 4 to 5 minutes or until heated through. For appetizers, quarter the muffins.

Museum of the North Beach

Desserts & Other Sweets

Icelandic Vinarterta

(Iceland)

Filling:

2 pounds prunes, cooked, pitted	½ teaspoon cardamom seeds, split
½ cup prune liquid	and ground
1 cup sugar	1 teaspoon vanilla, brandy or sherry

Chop prunes in food processor. Place chopped prunes in saucepan. Add liquid, sugar and cardamom. Cook on low heat, stirring often to prevent scorching, until as thick as jam. Cool. Add flavoring.

Cake:

1 cup butter	4 cups flour
1 cup sugar	2 teaspoons baking powder
2 eggs, slightly beaten	¼ cup milk
1 teaspoon vanilla	

Cream butter and sugar; blend in eggs and vanilla, beating until light and fluffy. Add sifted dry ingredients alternately with milk to creamed mixture. Dough should be firm but not stiff. Divide dough into 10 portions. Roll each portion to ¼ inch thick on lightly floured board to fit an 8-inch round cake pan. Turn cake pan upside down. Separately roll each portion of dough onto rolling pin to transport onto the bottom of an upside down ungreased cake pan; trim edges neatly. May use trimmings for more layers. Bake at 350° for 4 to 5 minutes until edge starts to brown. Cool layers on wire racks.

To Assemble:

Spread cooled filling on cooled layers. Press finished Vinarterta with palm of hand to make the many layers of cake blend with the filling. Wrap tightly in plastic wrap or aluminum foil. Let stand a day or so with a weight placed on the top of cake. Slice crusty edge from around entire cake; cut into 2-inch widths. Wrap in plastic wrap or aluminum foil. The widths freeze nicely. Remove from freezer an hour before serving and cut into ⅜-inch slices while still frozen.

Arnfridur Sigurdardottir
Nordic Heritage Museum

Flourless Chocolate Cake with Red Sky at Night Sauce

8 ounces (2 sticks) unsalted butter
16 ounces chopped dark chocolate
10 eggs, separated
Pinch salt
1½ cups sugar, divided

Preheat oven to 325°. Combine butter and chocolate in microwave-safe container. Heat in microwave 1 minute at a time, stirring between each minute, until chocolate and butter are incorporated and smooth. While chocolate is melting, whip egg whites and pinch of salt in mixer until peaks begin to form. Slowly add half the sugar to egg whites and keep whipping until whites form stiff peaks. Move egg whites to clean bowl. Combine yolks with remaining sugar and whip until yolks form ribbons. Add melted chocolate to yolks and mix well. Fold chocolate yolk mix into egg whites until incorporated. Pour into greased cake pan and bake 45 minutes or until the center seems set when wiggled.

Red Sky at Night Sauce:

20 ounces raspberries
2 cups sugar
½ cup water
½ cup Red Sky at Night wine from Westport Winery

Combine raspberries, sugar and water in saucepan over medium-high heat. Cook until reduced to 2 cups. Strain and continue cooking until reduced to 1 cup. Add wine, cook until thoroughly heated through. Spoon over cake when ready to serve.

Westport Winery

Chocolate Sadie Red Wine Cake

2 cups flour
¾ cup unsweetened dark cocoa
1¼ teaspoons baking soda
½ teaspoon salt
1 cup organic coconut oil
1¾ cups sugar

2 large eggs
1 teaspoon pure vanilla extract
1¼ cups red wine (Sadie Red is
    perfect for this cake)
Powdered sugar

Preheat oven to 350°. Butter and flour 12-inch Bundt pan. Combine flour, cocoa, baking soda and salt. In a large bowl cream coconut oil and sugar at medium-high speed until fluffy. Beat in eggs 1 at a time, then stir in vanilla. Working in two batches add in dry ingredients alternating with wine; mix well. Pour batter into prepared Bundt pan and bake 45 minutes. Cool 10 minutes. Remove from pan and dust with powdered sugar. Serve with vanilla ice cream or whipped cream.

Julie Salcido
Jacob Williams Winery

Jacob Williams Winery

3 Avery Road • Wishram
541-645-0462
www.JacobWilliamsWinery.com

Jacob Williams is a family-owned winery, named after the owner's two sons Jacob and William, and let's not forget about Sadie, the family dog. The delicious Red Blend (Sadie Red) continues to be the number one seller, year after year. As a boutique winery, the family has the flexibility to be creative, producing exceptional and limited quantity wines. The winemaker, John Haw, brings over 40 years of experience to the creation of Jacob Williams wine vintages. The Tasting Room is located in the Columbia Gorge, offering spectacular views of Mount Hood, the Columbia River, orchards, vineyards and beautiful rolling hills. Visit their tasting room, picnic on the patio, stroll through the vineyards and take in the scenery while enjoying award-winning wines.

Triple Chocolate Cake

1 box devil's food cake mix
1 (3.9-ounce) package chocolate
   instant pudding
1 cup sour cream
1 cup milk

½ cup water
½ cup vegetable oil
4 eggs
2 cups semisweet chocolate chips

Preheat oven to 350°. Grease and flour 10-inch Bundt pan. Combine all ingredients except chocolate chips. Beat 4 minutes then add chocolate chips. Pour into prepared pan and bake 40 to 50 minutes. Cool in pan 10 minutes then turn out onto wire rack to cool completely. Sprinkle with powdered sugar or glaze with chocolate ganache.

Rod Heikes
Pacific Days

Gluten-Free Chocolate Decadence Cake

1½ sticks (6 ounces) butter
12 ounces semisweet chocolate chips
8 eggs, beaten
⅔ cup sugar

Preheat oven to 350°. Melt together butter and chocolate chips, blend well and cool slightly; set aside. Beat eggs and sugar 10 minutes with electric mixer set to high or until light and fluffy. Fold in melted chocolate mixture until well blended. Pour into well-buttered springform pan lined with parchment paper. Cook 40 minutes. Cool completely before cutting. Serves 8.

J. J. Hills Fresh Grill
Icicle Village Resort

German Apple Cake

2 eggs, beaten
2 cups flour
2 cups sugar
1 teaspoon baking soda
1 cup vegetable oil
2 teaspoons cinnamon
1 teaspoon vanilla
Dash of salt
4 cups thinly sliced apples
½ cup chopped nuts (optional)

Combine all ingredients and blend by hand. Batter will be stiff. Spread into greased 9x13-inch pan. Bake at 350° for 45 to 60 minutes. Cool.

Cream Cheese Frosting:

2 (3-ounce) packages cream cheese, softened
3 tablespoons butter, melted
1½ cups powdered sugar
1 teaspoon vanilla

Combine all ingredients and mix until smooth. Smooth over cooled cake.

Cindy Simmons, Mother of Princess Brooke and Queen Shelby
Manson Apple Blossom Festival

Apple Cake

4 cups diced fresh apples
2 cups sugar
2 eggs, beaten
2 cups sifted flour

4 teaspoons cinnamon
1 teaspoon baking soda
1 cup chopped nuts

Cover apples with sugar and let stand until sugar is dissolved. Add eggs and mix to coat well. Add flour, cinnamon, baking soda and nuts. Bake in 9x13-inch pan at 350° for 30 minutes.

Sauce:

½ cup brown sugar
½ cup white sugar
½ cup water
¼ cup butter

1 teaspoon vanilla
¼ cup flour
¼ teaspoon salt

Mix Sauce ingredients in saucepan and bring to a boil. Cook until mixture thickens. Pour sauce over cake while sauce is still hot.

Barbara Fort Hisel, Queen 1943, Grand Marshal 1987
Manson Apple Blossom Festival

Oatmeal Cake

1 cup quick-cooking rolled oats
1 stick butter
1¼ cups boiling water
1 cup sugar
1 cup brown sugar
2 eggs

1⅓ cups flour
1 teaspoon baking soda
1 teaspoon cinnamon
½ teaspoon nutmeg
½ teaspoon salt

Place oats and butter in bowl; do not mix together. Pour boiling water over oats and butter and let stand 20 minutes. In separate large bowl, mix sugars and eggs. Add flour, baking soda, cinnamon, nutmeg and salt. Mix until well blended. Then add oats and butter; mix well. Pour into lightly greased 9x13-inch baking pan. Bake at 350° for 40 minutes. Cool completely.

Coconut Frosting:

6 tablespoons butter, melted
½ cup brown sugar
1 cup coconut

¼ cup evaporated milk
½ teaspoon vanilla

Combine all frosting ingredients; spread on cooled cake. Place under broiler until frosting bubbles and lightly browns.

Jan Callahan
Dachshunds on Parade

A Little More...

This is a great way to stretch a little dessert into a little more...

Any leftover cake broken into bite-size pieces (about half a cake)
4 cups fresh, frozen (thawed), or canned fruit (drained)
2 to 3 cups prepared whipped cream

Layer cake, fruit and whipped cream in a glass dish, repeating layers, ending with whipped cream. Garnish with fruit or chocolate shavings, if desired. Chill until ready to serve.

Ann Smith
Annual Holiday Tree Lighting

Annual Holiday Tree Lighting
Friday after Thanksgiving

100 Third Avenue • Pacific
www.pacificpartnerships.org

Pacific Partnerships Annual Holiday Tree Lighting event is a tradition that officially begins the holiday season each year in Pacific. There is holiday music to sing along to, an old-fashioned countdown to light the decorated Holiday Tree and free pictures with Santa! Seniors are on hand with hot cocoa, coffee and cookies to help keep holiday revelers warm. Bring a canned food donation for a chance to win a raffle prize, all food collected benefits the local food bank program.

Triple Threat Trifle

1 (9-ounce) box devil's food cake mix
2 (3.9-ounce) packages butterscotch instant pudding mix
½ cup Scatter Creek's Koko Indulgence port dessert wine, divided
1 (12-ounce) carton frozen whipped topping, thawed, divided
1 (12-ounce) jar butterscotch or caramel ice cream topping, divided

Prepare and bake devil's food cake according to package directions in an 8-inch square baking pan. Cool. Prepare pudding according to package directions. Cut cake into 2-inch cubes and place half in a 3-quart trifle bowl. Drizzle ¼ cup Koko Port onto cubed cake in bowl. Layer with half the whipped topping, half the pudding, and half the butterscotch or caramel topping. Repeat layers. Cover and refrigerate until serving. This delicious dessert is perfected when paired with a glass of Scatter Creek's Koko Indulgence port dessert wine!

Scatter Creek Winery

Sunset at the Woodland Tulip Festival

Huckleberry Pie

Huckleberries are a favorite northwest treat. They grow wild only in the northwest mountains and bears love them. This makes them a highly sought after commodity, sometimes selling for $40.00 a gallon.

4 cups huckleberries, divided
1¼ cups sugar
½ cup water
¼ cup cornstarch
1 tablespoon lemon juice
1 (9-inch) baked pie shell

In saucepan, cook 2 cups huckleberries with sugar, water, cornstarch and lemon juice. Cook until thickened. Cool completely. Add remaining huckleberries. Place huckleberry filling in baked pie shell.

Cream Cheese Mixture:

3 ounces cream cheese
½ cup powdered sugar
1 cup whipping cream, whipped

Blend cream cheese with powdered sugar until fluffy. Fold in whipped cream. Spread Cream Cheese Mixture on top of huckleberry filling. Chill.

Linda Shewey
Artisans at the Dahmen Barn

Favorite Dutch Apple Pie

Crust for Two Pies:

2 cups flour

¾ cup shortening

1 teaspoon salt

4 to 5 tablespoons milk

Combine all Crust ingredients, blending well. Divide into 2 parts, roll out and line pie plates.

Apple Filling for Two Pies:

6 to 7 tart apples, peeled, cored and
    sliced

½ cup sugar

½ teaspoon cinnamon

Combine all ingredients and pour into pie crusts.

Crumb Topping:

1½ cups flour

1 cup sugar

1¼ cups butter, softened

Blend until crumbly and sprinkle over top of apple filling. Bake 375° for 50 minutes until golden brown and apples are soft.

Jama England, Chairman
Manson Apple Blossom Festival

Apple Pie

Pie Crust:

1½ cups flour	1 cup shortening
½ teaspoon salt	½ cup ice water

Combine flour and salt in large bowl. Cut in shortening until mixture resembles coarse crumbs. Stir in ice water, 1 tablespoon at a time, until mixture forms a ball. Wrap dough in plastic wrap and refrigerate 2 hours. Sprinkle flour onto rolling surface. Divide dough in half and roll each to fit a 9-inch pie plate.

Filling:

8 cups peeled, cored and sliced assorted baking apples (Granny Smith works well)	¼ cup flour
	1 teaspoon ground cinnamon
	¼ teaspoon ground nutmeg
2 tablespoons lemon juice	2 tablespoons butter
¾ cup white sugar	1 egg yolk
¼ cup brown sugar	1 tablespoon milk

In large bowl, toss sliced apples with lemon juice. Combine sugars, flour, cinnamon and nutmeg; add to apples and toss well to coat. Press 1 pie crust into 9-inch pie plate and fill with apple mixture. Dot with butter. Place second crust on top of pie filling, cut slits in top of crust to vent. Seal edges with a fork or by hand. In small bowl, beat egg yolk and milk. Brush mixture over top crust. Bake at 425° for 15 minutes. Reduce heat to 350° and bake additional 40 minutes or until crust is golden and filling is bubbly.

Museum of the North Beach

Flat Apple Pie

Crust:

2½ cups flour
1 cup shortening
½ teaspoon salt

2 tablespoons sugar
1 egg yolk and milk to make ⅔ cup

Combine all Crust ingredients; mix well and divide in half. Roll out each thinly to the size of jelly-roll pan. Cover bottom of pan with 1 crust.

Filling:

2 cups cornflakes (optional)
6 to 8 apples, peeled, cored and
   sliced
1¼ cups sugar

½ teaspoon cinnamon
½ cup butter
1 egg white

Crush cornflakes and sprinkle over bottom crust. Add apples. Sprinkle with sugar and cinnamon; dot with butter. Top with second crust. Brush top of second crust with beaten egg white. Bake 375° for 45 to 50 minutes. While hot drizzle with Icing.

Icing:

¾ cup powdered sugar
Few drops of vanilla

Few drops of milk

Combine ingredients, mix well and drizzle on top of pie.

Mary England McFarlane, Princess 1969
Manson Apple Blossom Festival

Granny Smith Apple Pie

¼ cup plus 1 teaspoon sugar,
  divided
¼ cup packed brown sugar
1 tablespoon flour
1 teaspoon grated lemon peel
½ teaspoon ground cinnamon
¼ teaspoon ground nutmeg

6 medium Granny Smith apples,
  peeled, cored and sliced
1 cup raisins
1 (2-count) package refrigerated
  pie crusts
1 egg, beaten

Preheat oven to 450°. Spray 9-inch pan with nonstick spray. In a large bowl, combine ¼ cup sugar, brown sugar, flour, lemon peel, cinnamon and nutmeg; mix well. Add apples and raisins, stir until coated. Place pie crust into pan and form to pan; add apple mixture to pie pan. Cover with second pie crust. Seal and crimp edges together. Using a sharp knife cut steam vents into pie crust. Brush top of pie crust with beaten egg and sprinkle with sugar. Place on baking sheet and bake 40 minutes until apples are tender and pie crust is golden. Remove from oven and cool 30 minutes before serving.

Sedro-Woolley Loggerodeo

Lynden Pioneer Museum

Grandma Ester's Lemon Pie

Lemon Filling:

1 cup sugar

2 large eggs, separated (reserve egg whites)

Juice of 1 large lemon

½ teaspoon lemon zest

1½ cups water

3 tablespoons cornstarch

Combine sugar, egg yolks, lemon juice, lemon zest, water and cornstarch in saucepan. Cook over medium heat until thick. Remove from heat and set aside.

Meringue:

2 reserved egg whites

Dash cream of tartar

1 teaspoon sugar

Beat reserved egg whites with cream of tartar. Add sugar and beat until stiff.

1 baked pie shell

Fill pie shell with lemon filling, top with meringue and bake at 350° until top is brown (watch closely).

Sedro-Woolley Loggerodeo

Cherry Almond Pie

1 pie crust (store bought or homemade)
5 to 6 cups sour pie cherries, pitted, fresh
   or frozen
3 tablespoons flour

4 teaspoons cornstarch
4 teaspoons tapioca
1 teaspoon almond extract
1 teaspoon lemon juice

Preheat oven to 400°. Roll crust and place in a 9-inch deep-dish pie plate; flute edges. Combine cherries, flour, cornstarch, tapioca, almond extract and lemon juice; mix well. Pour into unbaked pie shell.

Topping:

1 cup flour
1 stick butter, softened

1 cup sugar
½ cup toasted almond slices

Combine Topping ingredients. Sprinkle evenly over pie filling. Place in 400° oven, centered, on lower rack. Bake 1 hour until golden brown and filling is bubbly.

Note: If using fresh cherries, add 1 cup sugar or to taste till just slightly sweetened.

Jenny Robelia and Laura Schip
Lone Pine Fruit & Espresso

Pumpkin Pie

Pumpkin pie can be made with any type of pumpkin, but the sweeter varieties are best. The small, round sugar pumpkins make excellent pies and are a perfect size if you only bake one or two pies. French pumpkins are sweeter and lighter in color, but they are also bigger. It does not take a very big pumpkin to make a pie. A 5-inch pumpkin will produce about 1 cup of purée.

Fresh pumpkin pies tend to be lighter in color than their canned pumpkin counterparts, but we think they have a fresher taste.

Grandma Carleton's Pie Crust:

1½ cups flour
Dash salt
½ cup shortening

4 tablespoons cold buttermilk or
    water

Combine flour and salt. Cut in shortening using a pastry blender or fork. Mixture should be crumbly and even. Add cold liquid all at once and stir. Knead with hands until smooth. Roll into a ball and press onto lightly floured surface. Roll out with rolling pin, alternating directions and turning over pastry each time it doubles in width. Be sure to keep the surface floured to prevent sticking. Roll until it is about 1-inch larger than 9-inch pie pan on all sides. Press pastry into pan and create an edge along rim by pressing the excess dough with your fingers.

Cooked Pumpkin:

Cut the pumpkin in half and scrape out seeds. Be sure to scrape off all stringy material as this will affect texture of the pie. Lay face down in roasting dish. Bake uncovered at 325° until very, very soft. Time varies depending on size of pumpkin. Separate pumpkin from skin; mash. Cooked pumpkin may be made ahead of time and refrigerated.

Filling:

¾ cup sugar
½ teaspoon salt
1 tablespoon cinnamon
1 teaspoon ginger

¼ teaspoon cloves
2 eggs
1¾ cups cooked pumpkin
1 (12-ounce) can evaporated milk

(continued)

Combine all dry ingredients in small bowl. Beat eggs lightly in separate, large bowl and stir in pumpkin. Add sugar mixture; gradually stir in evaporated milk. Pour into unbaked pie shell. Bake at 425° for 15 minutes. Reduce temperature to 350° and bake 45 to 50 minutes, or until toothpick inserted near center comes out clean. Cool before serving.

Carleton Farm

Carleton Farm

Farm Fresh Family Fun!

Farm Market open daily
May 1st through October 31st
10am to 7pm

630 Sunnyside Boulevard SE
Lake Stevens • 425-334-2297
www.carletonfarm.com

Carleton Farm is family owned and operated and located on 60 acres in Snohomish County north of Seattle. The vegetables grown on the farm are hand-picked and brought in ripe and ready for sale in the market. There is also a great selection of local meats, cheeses, wines, jarred products and other grocery items. Large quantities of produce are grown for canning and pickling.

Barn and tent space is available for birthday parties and family gatherings. The newly constructed Event Barn is available for weddings, company parties and other social events all season long.

The Fall Festival runs throughout October, with daily public access to the pumpkin fields and corn maze. Weekends offer hay rides, kid's play areas, delicious food from the Snack Shack and an opportunity to shoot a pumpkin out of custom made cannons! For chills and thrills, Carleton's 3 night-time venues in October are fun for the whole family. For more information visit Frightmaze.com.

Come shop locally and make great family memories at Carleton Farms! Find them Facebook for fun and informative updates.

No-Sugar-Added Black Cherry Mud Pie

12 sugar-free chocolate chip cookies, crumbled
2 tablespoons cocoa powder
1 cup melted butter
½ gallon no-sugar-added cherry ice cream, slightly thawed
Sugar-free chocolate syrup
Medium-size, round cookie cutter

In large bowl combine chocolate chip cookies, cocoa powder and melted butter. Mix well. Press evenly onto bottom of sheet pan to ¼- to ½-inch thickness. Place in freezer until set. Using cookie cutter, cut into 12 discs.

Press ice cream into bottom of sheet pan to 1-inch thickness. Set in freezer until set; cut into discs with cookie cutter.

Assemble in a trifle dish with the following layers; crust, ice cream, crust, ice cream, crust. Top with syrup.

Tony McGraw, Executive Chef, Pacific Beach Resort & Conference Center
2011 1st Place Winner
Chocolate on the Beach Festival

Triple Chocolate Crunch Pie

½ cup bittersweet chocolate chips
½ cup milk chocolate chips
½ cup white chocolate chips
1 (8-inch) pie crust, unbaked
½ cup brown sugar

½ cup corn syrup
3 eggs
1 egg yolk
1 teaspoon vanilla
1 cup chopped pecans (optional)

Preheat oven to 350°. Place all chocolate chips in pie crust. Mix brown sugar, corn syrup, eggs, egg yolk and vanilla. Pour over chocolate chips. Place pecans on top, if you wish. Bake 1 hour.

Extra: If desired, melt additional chocolate chips separately and drizzle on top of pie in fun designs.

Patricia Draheim, Owner, Paddies Perch
2010 1st Place Winner
Chocolate on the Beach Festival

Chocolate on the Beach Festival

Last Weekend in February

Pacific Beach • Moclips • Aloha • Copalis Crossing • Seabrook • Copalis Beach
www.chocolateonthebeachfestival.com

It's always raining chocolate the last weekend in February!

The small coastal community of Pacific Beach has been the home of the Chocolate on the Beach Festival since 2008. What has started out as a small museum fundraiser has now grown into a huge event for the communities of Moclips, Aloha, Copalis Crossing, Seabrook and Copalis Beach. The Festival is now a non-profit association supporting organizations and groups in the North Beach area with grants for historical, educational and community projects.

This fun, family festival offers something chocolate for everyone! Chocolate vendors, artists and crafters, cooking classes, recipe contests, eating contests and more! Attendees will find chocolate that is gluten-free, dairy-free, vegan, organic, fair trade, raw and even healthy stuff for their furry friends. Check them out at www.chocolateonthebeachfestival.com or on Facebook, and come join the fun, the last weekend in February.

Chocolate Chip, Peanut Butter & Oatmeal Cookies

1 cup butter
½ cup sugar
⅔ cup plus 2 tablespoons brown
   sugar
2 eggs
1 teaspoon pure vanilla extract
⅔ cup peanut butter

1½ cups flour
1 teaspoon baking soda
1 teaspoon salt
2 cups rolled oats
12 ounces Chocolate Necessities
   64% Guayaquil Chips

Cream butter and sugars, mix in eggs, vanilla and peanut butter. Add flour, baking soda, salt, oats and chocolate chips. Drop by rounded spoonfuls onto ungreased cookie sheets. Bake at 350° for 8 to 10 minutes.

Kevin G. Buck
Chocolate Necessities & Gelato

Harvest Chocolate Chip Cookies

½ cup butter, softened
½ cup shortening
¾ cup sugar
¾ cup brown sugar
1 egg
1 teaspoon baking soda
1 teaspoon cinnamon
1 teaspoon vanilla
½ teaspoon salt
1 cup canned pumpkin
3 cups flour
1 (8-ounce) package chocolate chips

Cream together butter, shortening and sugars. Add egg, baking soda, cinnamon, vanilla, salt and pumpkin. Gradually stir in flour. Fold in chocolate chips. Drop by large spoonfuls onto lightly greased cookie sheet. Bake at 350° for 9 to 10 minutes.

Butter Cookies

1 cup sugar
1 cup butter, softened
2 eggs

½ teaspoon baking powder
¼ teaspoon salt
3 to 3½ cups flour

Cream together sugar and butter; add eggs and mix well. In a separate bowl, combine baking powder, salt and flour. Add flour mixture to egg mixture a little at a time to make a medium-soft dough (you may not need it all). Chill dough for a least an hour. When ready to bake, fill a cookie press with dough and turn out cookies onto baking sheet. Bake at 350° for 8 to 10 minutes.

Lavender Shortbread Cookies

1½ cups butter, room temperature
⅔ cup sugar
2 tablespoons Pelindaba's Organic Culinary Lavender
2⅓ cups flour
½ cup cornstarch
¼ teaspoon salt
Pelindaba's Lavender Sugar for garnish

Preheat oven to 325°. Cover 2 baking sheets with parchment paper. In large bowl with electric mixer, cream together butter, sugar and lavender. Mix until light and fluffy, about 3 minutes. Add flour, cornstarch and salt; beat until combined. Divide dough in half. Flatten into squares and wrap in plastic. Chill until firm. On floured board, roll or pat out dough to thickness of ⅜ inch. Cut dough into 1½-inch squares or rounds. Transfer to baking sheets, spacing cookies 1 inch apart. Prick each cookie several times with a fork. Bake 20 to 25 minutes until pale golden (do not brown). Sprinkle with lavender sugar. Makes about 4 dozen.

Pelindaba Lavender®

Mercy Ingram's Scottish Shortbread

1 cup butter
½ cup sugar
2 plus cups flour, divided

Cut butter into sugar using 2 table knives. Add 1 cup flour and mix in. Sprinkle 1 cup flour on counter and add butter-sugar mixture. Start kneading dough like bread, adding in enough flour to stiffen dough. Divide in half and form into a rectangle about 3 inches wide and ½ inch thick. Poke dough rectangle with a fork clear through to the counter and down the total length. Cut across dough into finger-width pieces and place on ungreased baking sheet. Bake at 325° for 20 minutes or until golden brown.

Cool on rack and store in airtight container. Flavor develops when stored for several days if you can wait! Makes about 32 cookies.

Beth Wills, Mercy Ingram's granddaughter
Kelso Highlander Festival

Kelso Highlander Festival
Come and experience a "Wee Bit of Scotland"

2nd weekend in September

Tam O'Shanter Park • Kelso
360-423-0900
www.kelso.gov/visitors/highlander-festival

Each year the city of Kelso celebrates its Scottish roots with the Kelso Highlander Festival.

Activities include the Highland Dance Competition, team games, heavyweight events, fun run / walk, bagpipe performances, Scottish vendors, a parade, shortbread contest, and a gathering of the clans.

More than 4,000 people come to Tam O'Shanter park to dance, eat, shop and celebrate at this terrific free event. So put on your kilt and join one of the best Scottish gatherings in the country. Call or visit their site for yearly updated information.

Macaroons

3 egg whites
1 cup sugar
1 teaspoon vanilla

2 cups cornflakes
1 cup coconut
½ cup nuts, chopped

Beat egg whites, sugar and vanilla until very stiff. Gently fold in cornflakes, coconut and nuts. Drop by rounded spoonfuls onto cookie sheet and bake at 375° for 8 to 10 minutes or until lightly browned.

White Chocolate & Cranberry Cookies

1 cup butter, softened
1½ cups sugar
2 teaspoons baking soda
1 large egg
1½ cups flour

1½ cups quick-cooking rolled oats
1¼ cups coarsely chopped white
   chocolate
1½ cups cranberries, fresh or frozen

Cream together butter, sugar and baking soda in large bowl until creamy; beat in egg. Add flour, oats and white chocolate; mix well. Spoon dough in heaping tablespoons, 2-inches apart, on greased 12x15-inch baking sheet. Press 3 or 4 cranberries into each cookie. Bake at 350° until light golden, 10 to 12 minutes. Let cool on pans until firm to touch, about 2 minutes. With wide spatula, transfer to racks, cool completely. Serve or store airtight in refrigerator up to 2 days; freeze to store longer.

Museum of the North Beach

Angel Drop Sour Cream Cookies

1 cup sugar
½ cup shortening
2 eggs
½ cup sour cream
½ teaspoon baking soda

4 teaspoons baking powder
2½ cups flour
1 teaspoon vanilla
Sugar for topping

Preheat oven to 325°. Combine all ingredients except sugar for topping. Drop by rounded spoonfuls onto baking sheet. Bake 8 to 10 minutes. Watch carefully, these burn very easily. Sprinkle sugar on top while still hot.

Fun Fact

Washington became a state in 1889 and is the only state to be named after a US President. A portrait of George Washington appears on the state flag and also on the state seal.

Pelindaba's Lavender Chocolate Brownies

¾ cup butter, melted
1½ teaspoons vanilla extract
¾ cup flour
1½ cups sugar
½ cup cocoa powder

2 teaspoons Pelindaba's Organic
   Culinary Lavender
½ teaspoon salt
3 egg whites
½ cup chopped walnuts (optional)

Cream together butter and vanilla. In separate bowl, combine flour, sugar, cocoa powder, lavender and salt. Combine both wet and dry ingredients. Whip egg whites until foamy. Add egg whites to mixture. Add walnuts, if desired. Mix together well. Bake in greased 8x8-inch pan at 300° for 45 minutes. Check to make sure brownies are not overcooked. Serve with lavender ice cream or lavender whipped cream.

Pelindaba Lavender®

Pelindaba Lavender

Double Fudge Brownies

1½ cups sugar
¼ cup water
12 ounces chocolate chips
⅔ cup butter
2 teaspoons vanilla

4 eggs
1½ cups flour
½ teaspoon baking soda
½ teaspoon salt
1 cup chopped nuts

Combine sugar and water in saucepan; bring to a boil. Remove from heat and add chocolate chips, butter and vanilla, stirring until chocolate and butter melts. Add eggs, 1 at a time, to chocolate mixture. In separate bowl, combine flour, baking soda and salt. Add dry mixture to saucepan. Stir in chopped nuts. Bake in 9x13-inch pan at 325° for 30 minutes.

David Cross
Dachshunds on Parade

Katherine Hepburn Brownies

2 ounces unsweetened chocolate,
   coarsely chopped
½ cup unsalted butter, cut into
   pieces
1 cup sugar
½ teaspoon pure vanilla extract

2 large eggs
¼ cup flour
¼ teaspoon salt
1 cup chopped walnuts or pecans
   (optional)

Preheat oven to 325° and place rack in center of oven. Grease and flour 8x8-inch baking pan. Melt chocolate and butter in stainless steel bowl placed over a saucepan of simmering water (a double boiler can be used). Remove from heat and stir in sugar. Add vanilla extract and eggs. Add flour, salt and nuts. Pour into prepared pan and bake 30 to 35 minutes, or until toothpick inserted in center comes out clean. Remove from oven and cool on wire rack.

Museum of the North Beach

Sea Salty Caramel Brownies

½ cup white sugar
½ cup dark brown sugar
½ cup unsalted butter, softened
4 large eggs
1 teaspoon pure vanilla extract

1 cup flour
¼ teaspoon kosher salt
1 (15-ounce) can chocolate syrup
1 (11-ounce) jar Fran's classic caramel sauce
Coarse-ground sea salt

Preheat oven to 325° and prepare 9x13-inch glass baking dish by buttering lightly with unsalted butter and sprinkling with dry cocoa powder to coat; shake off excess.

Cream together sugars and butter until creamy and light brown. Add eggs, 1 at a time, blending well between each. Add vanilla. Gently stir in flour and kosher salt until no flour streaks remain.

Gently stir in a full can of chocolate syrup until no chocolate streaks remain. Pour into prepared baking dish and bake 50 minutes or until top spring backs lightly when touched. Cool on wire rack until just barely warm, drizzle with caramel sauce and sprinkle with sea salt. Cut into squares and serve with French vanilla ice cream topped with additional caramel sauce sprinkled lightly with sea salt.

Earla Harding
Foss Waterway Seaport

Foss Waterway Seaport

705 Dock Street • Tacoma
253-272-2750
www.fosswaterwayseaport.org

The Foss Waterway Seaport is located in the 1900 built historic Balfour Dock building and houses a Working Waterfront Maritime Museum, a 1-12 education center that includes on-water programs in marine and environmental science, various community events and programs with maritime themes, 1200 feet of transient moorage, and premier waterfront event rental space. The Seaport works with community groups, schools and the general public to provide exhibits and programs that highlight the history, the present vitality, and the future of Puget Sound and its connection to the people, the commerce, the environment and the ecology of the region. The Seaport will continue building renovations in phases through mid-2015. Visit the website to learn more about current activities happening at the Seaport.

Chocolate Brownies

1 stick butter, softened
1 cup sugar
4 eggs

1 (15-ounce) can chocolate syrup
1 cup flour
¾ cup chopped nuts

Preheat oven to 350°. Combine butter, sugar and eggs. Add syrup, flour and nuts; blend well. Pour into greased 10½x13-inch jelly-roll pan and bake 30 minutes.

Chocolate Frosting:

6 tablespoons butter
6 tablespoons milk

1½ cups sugar
½ cup chocolate chips

Place butter, milk and sugar into saucepan and heat over high heat, stirring constantly. Bring to full boil for 30 seconds, remove from heat and add chocolate chips. Beat with spoon until mixture just begins to thicken. Frosting should be consistency to pour (beating too long will make it like fudge). Spread over brownies.

Joan Fogelsonger
Annual Holiday Tree Lighting

Kenmore Air Harbor Bars

Graham crackers
1 cup dark brown sugar
1 cup butter
¾ cup quick-cooking oats

½ cup coconut
½ cup chopped nuts*
1 cup chocolate chips

Preheat oven to 375°. Grease an 11x15-inch jelly-roll pan. Line bottom of pan with graham crackers. In small saucepan, heat brown sugar and butter until well blended. Pour over graham crackers. Mix together oats, coconut, and nuts. Sprinkle over sugar mixture. Sprinkle chocolate chips over all. Bake 10 minutes. Cut and serve while warm.

*May substitute Rice Krispies if avoiding nuts due to allergy.

Kenmore Air Harbor

Kenmore Air Harbor

**Reservations 6am to 7pm daily
(Pacific Standard Time)**

**425-486-1257 • 866-435-9524
www.kenmoreair.com**

Three high school friends, reunited after World War II, founded Kenmore Air Harbor in 1946. With one airplane and a single hangar near a swamp at the North end of Lake Washington, Bob Munro, Reg Collins and Jack Mines created what was to become one of the largest and most respected seaplane operations in the world. Kenmore Air Harbor flies an eclectic mix of piston Beavers and turbine Otters and Caravans, landing passengers on glaciers, lakes and harbors. Kenmore Air Harbor continues to set the world standard by which floatplanes are judged, and is renowned for its superior expertise in plane maintenance and construction. The company's philosophy has remained unchanged since its establishment in 1946: "Do the Right Thing." Call or visit their website for reservations, charters and group sales, aircraft parts and service, and flight instructions.

Enchanted Apricot Bars

Shortbread:

½ cup butter, softened

½ cup brown sugar

1½ cups unbleached flour

Preheat oven to 350°. Cream together butter and brown sugar; add flour. Form into a ball and divide in half. Line a 7x11-inch baking dish with plastic wrap and press one ball into dish, spreading out to edges. Lift out plastic wrap with dough and set aside (this will be top layer). Lightly grease dish and press the remaining dough directly in bottom of dish.

Filling:

½ cup apricot preserves

1 teaspoon vanilla

½ cup brown sugar

1 cup coconut

½ cup chopped nuts (any type)

1 teaspoon baking powder

6 apricots

Powdered sugar

Combine preserves, vanilla, sugar, coconut, nuts and baking powder; mix well. Spread on shortbread in baking dish. Cut apricots in half; remove pit. Lay, inside down and evenly spaced, on top of filling mixture. Lay second shortbread dough on top of apricots. Press very gently around apricot halves. Bake 20 to 25 minutes. Remove from oven and sprinkle with powdered sugar. Cool completely and cut into squares. Each square should have 1 apricot half in middle.

Laura Schip
Lone Pine Fruit & Espresso

Apple Bars

Winner of the 2009 Manson Apple Blossom Festival Edible Apple Cookie Division

Bars:

¾ cup flour
½ teaspoon baking powder
¼ teaspoon baking soda
¼ teaspoon salt
½ teaspoon ginger
¼ teaspoon nutmeg
⅓ cup shortening

¾ cup sugar
2 large eggs
1 teaspoon fresh lemon zest
1 cup peeled, diced apples
½ teaspoon cinnamon
1½ teaspoons sugar

Preheat oven to 350°. Combine flour, baking powder, baking soda, salt, ginger and nutmeg; set aside. In a separate, large bowl, cream shortening and sugar. Beat in eggs and lemon zest. Gradually blend in dry mixture. Fold in apples. Spread dough evenly in ungreased 9-inch square baking pan. Combine cinnamon and sugar. Sprinkle evenly over dough. Bake 30 minutes or until firm. Let cool in pan on rack.

Lemon Icing:

½ cup sifted powdered sugar
1 teaspoon fresh lemon juice

Up to 1 teaspoon water

Combine all icing ingredients. Adjust to desired consistency. While Bars are still lukewarm, drizzle with icing. Cut into squares.

Betty Pettit, Chairman of Community Art Show and Headquarters
Princess 1957
Manson Apple Blossom Festival

Caramel Apple Oat Squares

20 caramels
1 (14-ounce) can sweetened
   condensed milk
1¾ cups flour
1 cup quick-cooking oats, finely
   blended in food processor
1½ cups brown sugar
½ teaspoon baking soda
½ teaspoon salt
1 cup butter
1 cup chopped walnuts (optional)
1 (21-ounce) can apple pie filling

Puyallup Fair Carmel Apples

Patrick Hagerty

Preheat oven to 375°. In heavy saucepan, over low heat, melt caramels with sweetened condensed milk, stirring until smooth. In large bowl, combine flour, oats, brown sugar, baking soda and salt; cut in butter until crumbly. Reserving 1½ cups crumb mixture, press remainder on bottom of 9x13-inch baking pan. Bake 15 minutes. Add nuts to reserved crumb mixture. Spoon apple pie filling over prepared crust; top with caramel mixture then reserved crumb mixture. Bake 20 minutes or until set. Cool, but very good warm with ice cream.

Lesa Lynn England, Secretary and Mother of Past Royalty
Manson Apple Blossom Festival

Apple Crisp

4 cups sliced tart apples
¼ cup water
1 teaspoon cinnamon
½ teaspoon salt

1 cup sugar
½ cup butter, softened
¾ cup flour

Spread apples in greased 8x8-inch baking pan. Sprinkle with water, cinnamon and salt. Combine sugar, butter and flour; mixture will be crumbly. Spread crumb mixture over apples. Bake, uncovered, at 350° for 40 minutes. Serve warm with ice cream.

Recipe can be doubled and baked in a 9x13-inch pan. Works great with Jonagolds, Goldens…pick your favorite tart apple.

Mary England McFarlane, Princess 1969
Manson Apple Blossom Festival

Aplets

1 cup finely grated apples
2 cups sugar
2 tablespoons Knox gelatin
5 tablespoons cold water

1 cup chopped nuts
½ teaspoon rose water
Powdered sugar

Combine apples and sugar, mix well. Place in saucepan and boil hard 1 minute. Reduce heat and simmer 30 minutes. Soak gelatin in cold water. Add gelatin water to hot pulp once completed simmering. Set aside to cool slightly. Add nuts and rose water. Pour into 8x8-inch pan. Set until cool and firm. Cut into squares and coat in powdered sugar by shaking squares in sack of powdered sugar.

Opal Fort, deceased, 1st generation volunteer
Manson Apple Blossom Festival

Apple Strudel

Crust:

½ cup milk
2 cups flour
1 teaspoon baking powder

½ teaspoon salt
2 tablespoons sugar
½ cup shortening

Add milk to dry ingredients and shortening; mix until easy to handle like pie crust. Sprinkle flour lightly on 2-foot piece of heavy foil. Roll dough out thinly on foil making a large rectangle.

Filling:

½ stick melted butter
6 small apples, peeled, cored and
    grated
¾ cup sugar

½ teaspoon cinnamon
Pinch of salt
2 tablespoons flour
Powdered sugar

Spread melted butter over dough. Combine grated apple with remaining ingredients and spread evenly over dough. Using foil, flip one third of dough over so two thirds of filling is encased with dough. Peel foil back from top of dough just flipped over. Using foil, flip last one third of dough over so all is encased in dough now. Peel back foil and seal edges. Move strudel still on foil onto a cookie sheet and bake at 350° for 40 minutes or until golden brown and the apples are soft. Sprinkle with powdered sugar.

Manson Apple Blossom Festival

Apple Dumplings for Four

Crust:

2 cups flour
1 teaspoon salt

⅔ cup oil
⅓ cup milk

Preheat oven to 425°. Combine all Crust ingredients, mixing well. Roll out on waxed paper. Place in 8x8-inch baking dish.

Filling:

4 small apples
⅓ cup sugar

1 teaspoon cinnamon
2 teaspoons butter, softened

Peel and core apples; set aside. Combine sugar, cinnamon and butter. Place apples on Crust. Fill each apple core with cinnamon mixture. Bring ends of pastry together over apples, overlap, moisten and seal.

Syrup:

⅔ cup sugar
1½ cups water

2 teaspoons butter
¼ teaspoon cinnamon

Combine all Syrup ingredients in saucepan over medium-high heat. Boil 3 minutes. Reserve ½ cup syrup and pour remainder in baking dish around bottom of dumplings (not on top). Bake at 350° for 40 to 45 minutes or until apples fork easily. Remove apples from oven and let set 30 minutes. Pour reserved syrup around dumplings. Serve with whipped cream or ice cream.

Janet Jones, Volunteer
Manson Apple Blossom Festival

Country Apple Dumplings

2 large Granny Smith apples, peeled and cored
2 (10-ounce) cans refrigerated crescent rolls
1 cup butter
1 cup sugar
½ cup brown sugar
1 can Mountain Dew

Preheat oven to 350°. Grease 9x13-inch baking dish. Cut each apple into 8 wedges and set aside. Separate crescent roll dough into triangles. Roll each apple wedge in crescent roll dough starting at smallest end. Pinch to seal and place in baking dish. Melt butter in small saucepan and stir in both sugars. Pour over apple dumplings. Pour Mountain Dew on top of dumplings. Bake 35 to 45 minutes or until golden brown.

Bayside Bed & Breakfast

The Vashion Island Coffee Roasterie

Napoleons with Summer Fruit

1 (17.3-ounce) package frozen puff pastry
3 pints assorted fresh summer fruit, raspberries, blueberries, blackberries,
    peaches, nectarines, etc.
2 (3.17-ounce) bars high-cocoa dark chocolate, chopped finely
Zest and juice of 1 lemon
1 cup heavy whipping cream

Preheat oven to 400° and line baking pan with parchment. Remove puff pastry from freezer and thaw until pliable.

Cut pastry sheets into 5x5-inch squares and cut each square in half again. Each rectangle will make 1 pastry so prepare only as many as you need. (Put remaining puff pastry sheets back into freezer.) Bake pastry rectangles on parchment-lined baking sheet 20 minutes or until puffed and golden brown. Place on rack to cool.

Lightly rinse and pat all fruit till completely dry. Set aside. Thinly slice any stone fruit (peaches, nectarines, apples, etc.) and brush with lemon juice to retard browning.

Beat heavy cream with mixer until stiff peaks form. Fold in lemon zest. Set aside in refrigerator.

When pastry is completely cool, remove from parchment sheet and cut each in half horizontally. Remove whipped lemon cream from refrigerator and spread first pastry half with layer of cream. Place layer of fruit on top of cream, top with another layer of cream and another layer of fruit. Place other half of pastry on top; set aside. Complete this process with each pastry. When all are complete, melt chocolate in microwave and drizzle on top of pastries and plate.

This delicate pastry is best served within a few hours of assembly and must be kept cool.

Lynn Andagan, Ocean Shores Bakery
Razor Clam Festival

Pear Clafouti

3 eggs
1¼ cups milk
½ cup flour
⅓ cup sugar
2 teaspoons vanilla
¼ teaspoon rum extract

⅛ teaspoon salt
⅛ teaspoon ground nutmeg
1 (29-ounce) can pears, drained and
   chopped
Whipped cream

Preheat oven to 350°. Beat eggs until foamy. Add milk, flour, sugar, vanilla, rum extract, salt and nutmeg. Beat at low speed until smooth. Spread pears in greased 10-inch quiche dish or pie plate. Pour batter over pears. Bake 50 to 60 minutes, or until knife inserted in center comes out clean. Let stand 15 minutes. Garnish with whipped cream.

Note: Clafouti is also excellent made with apples, peaches or blueberries.

Linda Lowber, loyal customer
Sunshine Farm Market

Strawberry Shortcake with Flaky Biscuits

4 cups flour
2 tablespoons sugar
1 tablespoon salt
1½ tablespoons baking powder
1 teaspoon baking soda

1 cup cold butter, cubed
1½ cups buttermilk
1 pint fresh strawberries, hulls
   removed and sliced
Whipped cream

Put all dry ingredients into mixing bowl. Using paddle attachment on mixer at low speed, mix together and slowly start adding cubed butter. Add buttermilk while on second speed, slowly a dough will start to form. Place onto floured surface and roll out about 1-inch thick. Cut out biscuits and bake at 400° for 12 minutes. Top with fresh strawberries and whipped cream.

Green Gables Inn

Raspberry Pretzel Dessert

2 cups crushed pretzels
1 tablespoon sugar
1 tablespoon melted butter
1 cup sugar
1 (8-ounce) package cream
   cheese, softened

1⅔ cups whipped topping
2 (3-ounce) packages raspberry
   gelatin
2 cups pineapple juice, warmed
1 (16-ounce) package frozen
   raspberries

Mix pretzels, sugar and butter. Press into greased 9x13-inch pan.
Bake at 400° for 7 to 10 minutes. Cool. Cream sugar and cream
cheese; fold in whipped topping. Spread over cooled pretzel crust.
Chill until firm. Dissolve gelatin in heated juice. Add raspberries.
When gelatin starts to thicken, pour over cream cheese layer. Chill
completely before serving.

Museum of the North Beach

Blueberry Cobbler

1¼ cups flour
½ cup sugar
¼ teaspoon salt
1½ teaspoons baking powder
¾ cup whole milk

⅓ cup butter, melted
2 cups fresh blueberries
⅓ cup sugar
1 teaspoon vanilla extract

Combine flour, sugar, salt and baking powder in large bowl; mix
well. Add milk and butter; stir to combine. Spread batter in a
greased 8x8-inch square baking pan. Sprinkle blueberries evenly
over batter. Sprinkle with sugar and drizzle with vanilla. Bake at
350° for 40 to 45 minutes.

Snicker Apple Delight

1 (5.9-ounce) package French vanilla instant pudding mix
1½ cups cold milk
1 (8-ounce) carton frozen whipped topping, thawed
6 apples, chopped (leave peel for color)
6 (2.07-ounce) Snicker candy bars, chopped

Beat or whisk pudding mix and milk, for 2 minutes. Let stand a few minutes until set. Gently fold in thawed topping until mixed well. Fold in chopped apples and Snicker bars. Refrigerate until ready to serve.

Janet Jones
Manson Apple Blossom Festival

Turtle Dessert

17 ice cream sandwiches
1 (12.25-ounce) jar caramel topping
1¼ cups chopped pecans, divided
1 (12-ounce) container frozen whipped topping, thawed, divided
¾ cup hot fudge topping, heated

Place 8½ ice cream sandwiches in a 9x13-inch baking dish. Spread evenly with caramel topping and sprinkle with 1 cup pecans. Top with 2 cups whipped topping. Top with remaining ice cream sandwiches. Spread remaining whipped topping evenly over sandwiches. Sprinkle with remaining ¼ cup pecans. Cover and freeze at least 2 hours. Let stand 5 minutes before serving; cut into squares. Drizzle with fudge topping.

Max's "Sticker Party Shock"

Max prepares this special treat for volunteers at the "sticker party," where name labels are affixed to bib numbers for all 50,000 participants.

1½ cups flour
½ teaspoon baking soda
½ teaspoon salt
1¼ sticks butter, softened
½ cup sugar
½ cup brown sugar, packed
1 egg

½ teaspoon vanilla extract
2 cups semisweet chocolate chips, divided
4 tablespoons peanut butter (may use chunky-style for variety)
1 to 2 cups crumbled Butterfinger or Nestlé Crunch bar

Preheat oven to 375°. In bowl mix flour, baking soda and salt; set aside. In separate bowl, beat butter and sugars to creamy consistency. Beat in egg and vanilla. Gradually stir in flour mixture. Stir in 1 cup chocolate chips. Spread batter evenly in lightly greased 12-inch pizza pan. Bake 20 to 24 minutes or until lightly browned. Immediately sprinkle remaining chocolate chips over cookie and spoon peanut butter on top of chocolate chips. As chips soften, use knife or spatula to blend the two into a frosting-like mixture, spreading evenly. Sprinkle crumbled candy bar on top of warm frosting.

Max Bischoff, Board Member
Lilac Bloomsday Run

Jeff Ferguson

Lilac Bloomsday Run

May

12-kilometer run/walk • Spokane
509-838-1579 • www.bloomsdayrun.org

The Lilac Bloomsday Run is one of America's classic road races. Founded by Olympic marathoner Don Kardong during the running boom that swept the nation in the late 1970s, the first Bloomsday was held on May 1, 1977 with over 1,000 runners participating. Since then, Bloomsday has grown to attract nearly 50,000 entrants each year, with world-class racers competing for prize money while back-of-the-packers enjoy a seven-and-a-half-mile walk with friends, family and neighbors, navigating a course that weaves back and forth across the Spokane River gorge. Nearly 30 entertainers create a festive atmosphere along the route, while the chance to earn a coveted Bloomsday finisher's T-shirt—the color and design of which are kept secret until the finish—keeps participants of all abilities moving toward the dramatic finish line above the falls in downtown Spokane.

Lentil Love Sticky Toffee Pudding

Winner of the "I Hate Lentils" award 2011 Legendary Lentil Cook-Off.

4 ounces dates, pitted and chopped
½ teaspoon baking soda
1 cup boiling water
1½ cups salted butter, divided
2 cups sugar
2 eggs

1 cup cooked lentils, unseasoned
¼ teaspoon salt
3 cups cake flour
2½ cups dark brown sugar
3 cups whipping cream, divided
¼ cup powdered sugar, sifted

Preheat oven to 350°. Spray 9x13-inch baking dish with butter-flavor nonstick cooking spray; set aside.

In a small bowl, stir together dates and baking soda. Pour water over mixture. Cover bowl and set aside 15 minutes.

In a large bowl, cream ½ cup butter and sugar until light and fluffy. Mix in eggs, lentils and salt. Fold in flour and prepared dates. Pour batter into prepared pan and bake 30 to 40 minutes, or until tests done.

In medium saucepan, over medium-high heat, mix together remaining butter, brown sugar and 2 cups cream; bring to boil. Poke holes in baked cake and pour half of sauce on cake.

Whip remaining 1 cup cream until soft peaks form; add powdered sugar. Continue whipping cream until stiff peaks form. Cut cakes into squares. Serve with remaining warm sauce and whipped cream.

Helen Fields
National Lentil Festival

Zinfandel Ice Cream

2 bottles Maryhill Reserve Zinfandel
2 cinnamon sticks
½ teaspoon whole black peppercorns
2 cups milk
2 cups heavy cream
1¼ cups sugar, divided
9 egg yolks
¼ teaspoon kosher salt
⅛ teaspoon vanilla extract

Pour wine into a large pot and bring to simmer. Add cinnamon sticks and peppercorns. Simmer until wine is reduced to 1 cup, about 1 hour. In a large pan, bring milk, cream and ¾ cup sugar to a boil and turn off heat. In a separate bowl, whisk together egg yolks and remaining sugar. Temper yolks into boiling milk by gradually whisking about 1 cup milk into yolks and adding this back into the pot with remaining milk. Stir in salt and vanilla. Whisk in reduced wine. Set pan over a bowl full of ice to cool. Pour chilled ice cream base through fine mesh strainer. Process base in an ice cream maker according to manufacturer's directions. Chill at least 2 hours before serving.

Maryhill Winery

Lavender Ice Cream

1 cup half-and-half
2 cups heavy cream
1 teaspoon dried lavender placed in a tea ball or gauze
7 egg yolks
¾ cup honey

Pour half-and-half and cream into a heavy saucepan. Add lavender and warm about 5 minutes. Remove lavender. Whisk egg yolks in bowl until frothy. Slowly pour half the warm cream into egg yolks while whisking continuously. Add yolk and cream mixture into saucepan with remaining half of warm cream and continue to heat on low, stirring constantly, for about 5 minutes. Strain mixture into a bowl and whisk in honey. Chill mixture and then freeze according to the instructions on ice cream maker.

Springtime Bloom Ohme Gardens

Chocolate Sea-Salted Smoky Almond Bark

1 (16-ounce) bar baking chocolate
1 cup coarsely chopped smoked almonds, divided
Large-crystal sea salt

Line two 8x8-inch pans with parchment paper; set aside. Microwave chocolate on high 1 minute. Microwave an additional 10 to 15 seconds, if necessary, stirring just until smooth. Stir in ½ cup almonds. Pour into pans and sprinkle with remaining almonds, tapping pan to settle nuts. Cool slightly then sprinkle with sea salt. Refrigerate 1 hour or until firm. Break into pieces. Can be stored in an airtight container at room temperature for several days.

Glenda White
Pacific Days

Chocolate Ganache

2 cups crème (heavy cream)
12 ounces Organic Colombian 65% chocolate chips

Warm crème to temperature right before boiling. Do not boil. Remove from heat. Add chocolate chips. Stir until all chips have melted. Serve over vanilla ice cream.

Chocolate Necessities & Gelato

Index

Washington State Flower:
Rhododendron macrophyllum

Index of Events & Destinations

This Index is meant to be a tool for locating all events and destinations featured in *Eat & Explore Washington*. Each event or destination is listed by both name and city referencing the page number for its featured page. Events and destinations that have a recipe are additionally listed by event or destination name then recipe, referencing the page number for the recipe. A complete Index of Recipes begins on page 237.

Benny, Sunshine Farm Market

Index of Recipes

South Sound BBQ Festival

Puyallup Fair Corn

Philip Palermo

P

Westport Art Festival

Robert Karl Cellars

Recipe Notes

Travel Plans

About the Author:

In 1999, Christy Campbell began her journey in the world of cookbooks when she took a position at a publishing company specializing in regional cookbooks. At the time, it was an all-new experience, so she immersed herself in cookbooks, both at home and at the office. With the help of the associate publisher and her personal mentor, Sheila Simmons (author, STATE HOMETOWN COOKBOOK SERIES), Christy learned the in's and out's of the small press world, devoting herself to cookbooks for the next 6 years. After the birth of her youngest son, Campbell took a sabbatical from the publishing world to focus on her young family.

In 2009, Campbell reconnected with Sheila Simmons and began work with Great American Publishers, reenergizing a 10 year love of cookbooks. She is now an integral part of Great American Publishers and has begun a new cookbook series of her own. The EAT & EXPLORE STATE COOKBOOK SERIES chronicles the favorite recipes of local cooks across the United States while highlighting the most popular events and destinations in each state.

When she is not writing cookbooks, selling cookbooks or cooking recipes for cookbooks, Christy Campbell enjoys volunteering at her children's school, running and reading. She lives in Brandon, Mississippi, with her husband Michael and their two sons.

State Hometown Cookbook Series
A Hometown Taste of America, One State at a Time

EACH: $18.95 • 240 to 272 pages • 8x9 • paperbound

The STATE HOMETOWN COOKBOOK SERIES captures each state's hometown charm by combining great-tasting local recipes from real hometown cooks with interesting stories and photos from festivals all over the state. As a souvenir, gift, or collector's item, this unique series is sure to take you back to your hometown... or take you on a journey to explore other hometowns across the country.

Georgia Hometown Cookbook • 978-1-934817-01-8

Louisiana Hometown Cookbook • 978-1-934817-07-0

Mississippi Hometown Cookbook • 978-1-934817-08-7

South Carolina Hometown Cookbook • 978-1-934817-10-0

Tennessee Hometown Cookbook • 978-0-9779053-2-4

Texas Hometown Cookbook • 978-1-934817-04-9

• Easy to follow recipes produce great-tasting dishes every time.

• Recipes use ingredients you probably already have in your pantry.

• Fun-to-read sidebars feature food-related festivals across the state.

• The perfect gift for anyone who loves to cook.

• Makes a great souvenir.

Family Favorite Recipes

It's so easy to cook great food your family will love with 350 simply delicious recipes for easy-to-afford, easy-to-prepare dinners. From **Great Grandmother's Coconut Pie**, to **Granny's Vanilla Wafer Cake**, to **Mama's Red Beans & Rice**, this outstanding cookbook is the result of decades of cooking and collecting recipes. It's so easy to encourage your family to eat more meals at home...to enjoy time spent in the kitchen... to save money making delicious affordable meals...to cook the foods your family loves without the fuss...with *Family Favorite Recipes*.

$18.95 • 248 pages • 7x10 • paperbound • 978-1-934817-14-8

www.GreatAmericanPublishers.com • www.facebook.com/GreatAmericanPublishers

Eat & Explore Cookbook Series

EAT AND EXPLORE STATE COOKBOOK SERIES is a favorite of local cooks, arm-chair travelers and cookbook collectors across the United States. Call us toll-free **1.888.854.5954** *to order additional copies or to join our Cookbook Club.*

EACH: **$18.95 • 240 to 272 pages • 7x9 • paperbound**

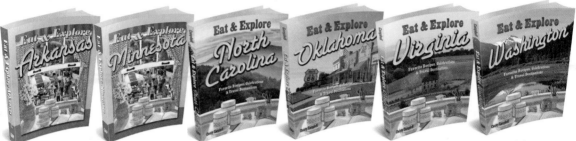

Arkansas	Minnesota	North Carolina	Oklahoma	Virginia	Washington
978-1-934817-09-4	978-1-934817-15-5	978-1-934817-18-6	978-1-934817-11-7	978-1-934817-12-4	978-1-934817-16-2

Don't miss out on our upcoming titles—join our Cookbook Club and you'll be notified of each new edition.

www.GreatAmericanPublishers.com • www.facebook.com/GreatAmericanPublishers

ORDER FORM

Mail to: Great American Publishers • P. O. Box 1305 • Kosciusko, MS 39090
Or call us toll-free 1.888.854.5954 to order by check or credit card

❏ Check Enclosed
Charge to: ❏ Visa ❏ MC ❏ AmEx ❏ Disc

Card #

Exp Date   Signature

Name

Address

City   State

Zip

Phone

Email

Qty.   Title   Total

Subtotal

Postage ($3 first book; $0.50 each additional)

Total